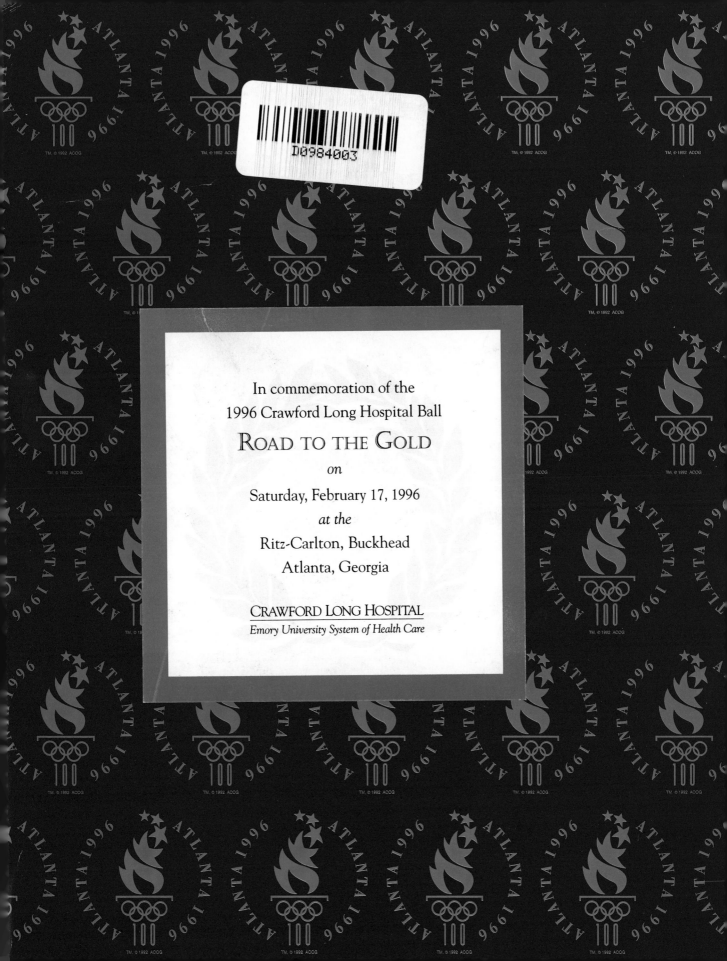

In commemoration of the
1996 Crawford Long Hospital Ball

ROAD TO THE GOLD

on

Saturday, February 17, 1996

at the

Ritz-Carlton, Buckhead
Atlanta, Georgia

CRAWFORD LONG HOSPITAL
Emory University System of Health Care

GOOD AS GOLD

CENTENNIAL OLYMPIC GAMES COOKBOOK

GOOD AS

GOLD

CENTENNIAL
OLYMPIC GAMES
COOKBOOK

AMERICA'S FINEST CHEFS
AND FAMOUS COOKS
CELEBRATE 100 YEARS OF THE
MODERN OLYMPIC GAMES

FAVORITE RECIPES® PRESS
A DIVISION OF SOUTHWESTERN/GREAT AMERICAN, INC.
Nashville, Tennessee

To order additional copies, please call Favorite Recipes ® Press.

Copyright ©1995 by Favorite Recipes ® Press
Publishing division of Southwestern/Great American, Inc.
P.O. Box 305142, Nashville, Tennessee 37230
1-800-358-0560

Conceived, edited, and published under the direction of:

Ralph Mosley	Chairman of the Board
Tom McDow	President and Publisher
Dave Kempf	Vice President of Sales
Roger Conner	Regional Sales Manager and Executive Editor

Good As Gold

Managing Editor	Mary Cummings
Project Editor	Ronald Kidd
Food Editor	Charlotte Walker
Sports Essayist	Dwight Chapin
Other Text	Yvonne Martin Kidd
Book Design	Bruce Gore
Art Direction	Bud Schatz
Food Photography	Ron Manville
Food Styling	James Griffin
Typography	Ginny Schatz, Bud Schatz, Barbara Teeslink
Production	John Moulton
Research	D. Fran Morley
Test Kitchen	Charlene Sproles
Nutritional Profiles	James Scheer, RD, DO; Debbie Van Mol, RD

ISBN 0-87197-440-1
Library of Congress Catalog Number LC-00000

Manufactured in the United States of America
First printing: 1995

OVERLEAF: *Bob Methias (London, 1948)*
INSET: *Dean Fearing's "Skillet-Fried Corn Bread with Spicy Shrimp & Crab Meat" (page 129)*

PHOTO AND ILLUSTRATION CREDITS: *Front cover, back cover (top)* Yum, Inc.; *back cover (bottom)* courtesy Dean Fearing; *2-3* AP/Wide World; *3 (inset)* Yum, Inc.; *5* A. Hubrich/H. Armstrong Roberts; *6 (top)* Hulton Deutsch/ALLSPORT; *6 (bottom)* courtesy Atlanta Centennial Olympic Properties; *7* Yum, Inc., china courtesy Ross Simons Jewelers, Providence, RI; *8 (left)* courtesy Charles Carroll; *8 (right)* courtesy Dean Fearing; *9 (top)* courtesy Michael Cordua; *9 (bottom left)* courtesy Ann Amernick; *9 (bottom middle)* courtesy Robert Del Grande; *9 (bottom right)* courtesy John Folse; *10-11* Vandystadt/ALLSPORT; *13* Hulton Deutsch/ALLSPORT; *14 (left)* ALLSPORT; *14 (right)* courtesy Atlanta Centennial Olympic Properties; *15, 16 (left, right), 17* AP/Wide World; *18, 19 (left)* Tony Duffy/ALLSPORT; *19 (right)* Bob Martin/ALLSPORT; *20 (left, right)* AP/Wide World; *21* Richard Martin/ALLSPORT; *23* courtesy Atlanta Centennial Olympic Properties; *24 (left)* courtesy Atlanta Chamber of Commerce; *24 (top, bottom right), 25* Atlanta Centennial Olympic Properties; *26* Ken Levine/ALLSPORT; *27* courtesy Atlanta Centennial Olympic Properties; *28-29* Yum, Inc., china courtesy Ross Simons Jewelers, Providence, RI; *30 (top left)* courtesy Cory Schreiber; *30 (bottom left)* courtesy Fred Halpert/Kingmond Young Photography; *30 (top middle)* courtesy Marcel Desaulniers; *30 (bottom middle)* courtesy Johnny Rivers/The Walt Disney Company; *30 (right)* courtesy Emily Luchetti; *31 (left)* courtesy Michael Cordua/Kevin McGowan, photographer; *31 (middle)* courtesy Donna Nordin; *31 (right)* courtesy Cassandra Mitchell; *202* courtesy International Center for Sports Nutrition; *203 (left)* courtesy U.S. Department of Agriculture, Human Nutrition Information Service; *203 (right)* L. Powers/H. Armstrong Roberts.

Jacques Pépin's recipes reprinted by permission from *Happy Cooking!* by Jacques Pépin, published by KQED Books.

We gratefully acknowledge the assistance of the McDonald's Corporation, the International Center for Sports Nutrition, and Atlanta Centennial Olympic Properties, as well as all the chefs and their staffs who participated.

*Dedicated to the athletes
of the Centennial Olympic Games*

C O N T

E   N   T   S

PART II THE RECIPES

Atlanta 1996

A Celebration of Excellence

WHY WOULD OVER FIFTY of America's finest chefs and famous cooks join in this tribute to the one hundredth anniversary of the Modern Olympic Games? What is so magnetic and inspiring about the Olympic Games that they warrant this special salute?

Charles Carroll

There are many things about the Games that capture our attention and call for celebration: the excitement of the competition, the stories behind the scenes, the sheer beauty of the spectacle.

Above all, though, the Olympic Games are a monument to the human spirit and its drive for excellence. The Games show us how—with dedication, discipline, and unwavering perseverance—anything is possible.

In athletics, excellence might consist of grace on a balance beam, speed on the track, or strength on the wrestling mat. But excellence isn't limited to sports. It reaches into every occupation and avocation imaginable—from childcare to higher education; medicine to math; music to

Dean Fearing's "Butterfinger Candy Bar Pie" (page 130)

art; quilt making to carpentry. And it extends into kitchens across the country.

All the chefs and cooks taking part in this tribute, like the athletes who will compete in Atlanta and those who have gone before, have proven themselves to be the best of the best. All proudly boast awards bestowed by peers and patrons. Whether the owner and cook of a small cafe serving up freshly baked Southern biscuits with homemade blackberry preserves or a culinary academy graduate with an international reputation for exquisite French pastry, each is a world-class contender.

Michael Cordua's "Hongos Rellenos" (page 121)

As these talented chefs and cooks salute the Centennial Olympic Games by presenting special menus adapted for home use, they remind us that with hard work and discipline, each of us can apply our own unique gifts and talents to the pursuit of excellence. And that is a cause worth celebrating.

Ann Amernick

Robert Del Grande

John Folse

PART I

THE GAMES

· · · · · · · · · · · ·

100 Years of Gold

A New Beginning

1896 Olympic Games poster

THE BARON KNEW BEST. "The Olympic Games symbolize an entire civilization, superior to countries, cities, military heroes, or even the ancient religions," he said. "The Olympic Games—the entire planet is their domain—all sports, all nations."

No one could ever accuse Baron Pierre de Coubertin, a French nobleman, of thinking small. More than anyone, his vision was responsible for the Modern Olympic Games.

While still a military cadet, he had studied the ancient Olympic Games in Olympia, Greece, which began as a tribute to the Greek god Zeus in 776 B.C. and continued every four years for more than a thousand years, until they were banned by Emperor Theodosius in 393 A.D. Baron de Cou-

Baron Pierre de Coubertin

bertin became obsessed with the idea that the Games should resume. He was aware of aborted attempts to re-start them by a Greek named Evangelios Zappas in 1859 and again in 1870. But de Coubertin was undeterred. He sought support from sports federations and leaders around the world.

"Let us export oarsmen, runners, fencers," he told them. "There is the free trade of the future—and on the day when it shall take its place among the customs of Europe, the cause of peace will have received a new and powerful support. So please help me reestablish the Olympic Games."

The sales pitch worked. The Modern Olympic Games returned in 1896, in Athens. The first gold medal in more than fifteen centuries went to American James Connolly, a Harvard freshman who managed a distance of 45 feet in the hop, step, and jump. Greece smiled when one of its own, a peasant named Spiridon Loues, after fasting and prayers, took the marathon—which quickly became the Modern Olympic Games' most dramatic and spectacular event. Loues's victory was such a big deal with the home folks that the Crown Prince of Greece and his brother carried Loues on their shoulders to the royal box to receive a trophy from a beaming King George. Loues later was showered with money and presents, even offered free meals, clothing, and haircuts for life. In the true spirit of the Olympic Games, he turned down everything but a horse and cart, to take water to his village.

Except for the war years of 1916, 1940, and 1944, the Olympic Games have survived. And, despite political disputes, most of the time they've been all sports, all nations.

OVERLEAF: *Wilma Rudolph, right (Rome, 1960)*

Men's Track and Field

IT BEGAN, MORE OR LESS, with Jim Thorpe, who had a memorable exchange with King Gustav V of Sweden after winning the decathlon at the 1912 Olympic Games in Stockholm. "Sir, you are the greatest athlete in the world," Gustav said, handing Thorpe a bronze bust of himself. "Thanks, king," Thorpe answered, perhaps changing royal protocol forever.

It continued, through the decades, to the 1976 Games in Montreal, where Bruce Jenner picked up an American flag after winning the decathlon and raced around the stadium.

There have been myriad memorable moments in men's track and field at the Olympic Games. The total dominance of the distance events by Finland's Paavo Nurmi (nine gold medals, three silvers) in the 1920s. The "salute" by African American Jesse Owens to Germany's Adolf Hitler— four gold medals at the 1936 Games in Berlin. American Bob Beamon's historic long jump of 29 feet, 2 1/2 inches at Mexico City in 1968. Ethiopian Abebe Bikila's triumphs in the marathon in 1960 and 1964, the first of them run barefooted, the second run forty days after an appendectomy. A fateful fall by American Jim Ryun in a 1,500-meter heat at Munich in 1972.

Bruce Jenner (Montreal, 1976)

Four gold medals by American Carl Lewis, the nonpareil modern athlete, at Los Angeles in 1984. Canadian sprinter Ben Johnson's disqualification over steroid use in 1988 at Seoul.

But, as much as anything, men's track has been defined by the decathlon, from Thorpe to Great Britain's Daley Thompson, and all the great Americans in between: Glenn Morris, Bob Mathias, Milt Campbell, Rafer Johnson, Bill Toomey, Bruce Jenner.

Central Californian Mathias, a double winner of the event, in 1948 at London and 1952 at Helsinki, still stands out. He was just seventeen years old in '48, the youngest person ever to make the U.S. track team in the Olympic Games; and, amazingly, he had competed in the decathlon for only three months. "Nobody expected me to do anything," he said. "I'd never even been out of California before." He was also too young to feel much pressure. To him, the Olympic Games just seemed like a big track meet. When he won, he was the youngest male ever to take a gold medal in track. Neither of his victories was easy. After the second, he realized what he'd done. "The stadium in Helsinki was full," he said, "the people were cheering, and I soaked it in. It was wonderful. It wasn't a dream anymore. I'd really done it."

Women's Track and Field

SHE COULD DO ANYTHING as an athlete. Hit a golf ball. Pitch a baseball. Shoot a basketball. Swing a tennis racquet. Throw the shot and discus, jump the hurdles and the high jump bar, and hurl the javelin. Texan Babe Didrikson was voted the finest female athlete of the first fifty years of the twentieth century. None better has come along since. In 1932, at the Los Angeles Games, she set a standard for female Olympic track-and-field athletes. She won gold medals in the 80-meter hurdles and the javelin throw and what should have been a gold in the high jump. Didrikson was penalized for "diving" over the bar and placed second, even though she had cleared a world record height of 5 feet, 5 3/4 inches. Even more remarkably, she had qualified for five events in the 1932 Olympic Games. The prevailing rules limited her to only three.

Florence Griffith Joyner (Los Angeles, 1984)

Didrikson has had many worthy successors. Fanny Blankers-Koen of Holland, who won four of the nine women's track-and-field events in 1948. Iolanda Balas of Romania, a double gold medal in the high jump in the 1960s. Massive Tamara Press of the Soviet Union, whose stunning shot put victory in '60 and shot-discus double in '64 were tarnished when she later decided to skip sex tests. A lustrous line of American sprinters, including Wyomia Tyus, Evelyn Ashford, and the flamboyant Florence Griffith Joyner. Heptathlete Jackie Joyner-Kersee, who in the last decade has been as dominant in women's track as four-time Olympian Carl Lewis has on the men's side.

Perhaps no female has symbolized the Olympic Games ideal the way sprinter Wilma Rudolph did. The twentieth child in a Tennessee

Mildred "Babe" Didrikson, far right (Los Angeles, 1932)

family of twenty-two, Rudolph was stricken by illnesses, including a mild form of polio when she was four, and her left leg was paralyzed. Her parents were told she might not walk again. They massaged her legs three or four times a day, and she did walk, but it was with a special shoe she had to wear until she was eleven. Five years later, she was a member of the U.S. Olympic Team and won a bronze medal in Melbourne. At the 1960 Games, in Rome, she became the first American woman to win three track-and-field gold medals. Her power and grace—that magnificent surge to the tape—still fill the mind, nearly four decades later.

Atlanta 1996

Men's Swimming and Diving

ONE JOURNALIST SAID he looked like a cross between Omar Sharif and the Marlboro Man. One thing was sure. You couldn't miss handsome,

Mark Spitz (Munich, 1972)

mustachioed Mark Spitz in 1972, his seven gold medals from Munich covering his chest on magazine covers around the world. Seven was a lucky number for Spitz that early fall. He entered seven events, won all of them, and set seven world records. Unfortunately, Spitz didn't get to celebrate his triumph in Germany. Because terrorists had invaded the Olympic village and killed Jewish athletes, it was feared that Spitz, who was Jewish, would also be a target. He was flown back to the U.S. early. "When competition resumed after the killings," he said, "I was back home in Sacramento, watching the replays of my races as if they were that night's highlights."

Spitz is the top medal man in Olympic Games swimming history, but there have been many other stars, beginning with Hawaiian Duke Kahanamoku in 1912 and 1920 and Tarzan-to-be Johnny Weismuller, who won five golds in 1924 and 1928. Names like Don Schollander, Murray Rose, Michael "The Albatross" Gross, Roland Matthes, John Naber, and Pablo Morales followed. Then came 6-foot-6-inch Californian Matt Biondi, who finished his career with one fewer gold medal than Spitz, but at Barcelona in 1992 became the first male swimmer to win gold in three Olympic Games. Biondi scored five of those medals at Seoul in 1988.

Without question, the preeminent male diver in Olympic Games history— with apologies to American Sammy Lee and Italian Klaus Dibiasi—is Greg Louganis, who escaped a troubled childhood by diving again and again into a pool. He was favored to win two gold medals at Moscow in 1980 but couldn't compete because of the U.S. boycott. Undaunted, he displayed astonishing grace and a competitor's heart in taking double golds both at Los Angeles in 1984 and Seoul in 1988. To win in '88, he had to survive what could have been a severe injury, when his head struck the springboard. For his first dive after the mishap, he was awarded 87.12 points, the highest score given for any diver in the preliminaries.

At Barcelona in 1992, American Mark Linzi won the springboard competition, giving the U.S. a remarkable fifteen of nineteen gold medals in that event since it was first included in the Olympic Games.

Women's Swimming and Diving

Australian Dawn Fraser made waves—lots and lots of them. In the pool, as far and away the best female swimmer of her time, she won a total of four gold medals and four silvers in the 1956, 1960, and 1964 Olympic Games. Out of the pool, she clashed with all kinds of people, from Australian team officials to her teammates, mainly over failure to conform to team rules. But, more than anything, she had remarkable perseverance. While driving in Australia in 1964, her car skidded and slammed into a parked truck. Her mother was killed, and Fraser had to spend six weeks with her neck in a cast because of a chipped vertebra. Only seven months later, at the advanced swimming age of twenty-seven (her teammates nicknamed her "Granny"), she won her third gold medal in the 100-meter freestyle.

Tracy Caulkins (Los Angeles, 1984)

Americans such as Debbie Meyer, Claudia Kolb, and Donna de Varona performed very well in the 1960s, too. But then came a dominant wave of broad-shouldered East Germans such as Kristin Otto and Kornelia Ender (who along with her husband, Roland Matthes, won sixteen swimming medals).

U.S. coaches produced some sterling female swimmers, too, including Tracy Caulkins of Nashville, who added three 1984 gold medals to the more than sixty U.S. records she'd set, and Janet Evans and Summer Sanders, who had competed together briefly at Stanford University. After winning the third of her three golds at Seoul in 1988, Evans giggled in delight and said, "I'm smiling because I'm having fun. That's what this is all about, to have fun." The normally cheery and composed Sanders didn't have fun in Barcelona in 1992, because of what she saw as unrealistic expectations. She won two golds, a silver, and bronze, but said, "I don't think anyone realizes how much pressure there is. Swimming should be simple. We all make it too complex."

In women's diving, America's early successes with competitors such as Vicki Draves, Pat McCormick (who won double golds in springboard and platform diving in 1952 and 1956, the last two just eight months after giving birth to a baby boy), and Micki King, gave way to the world. Moving front and center in the last decade have been the Chinese, led by athletes such as tiny (5-foot-1, 92-pound) Zhou Jihong, who listened to piano concertos on headphones between dives and won a 1984 gold medal, and Xu Yanmei, a star of the 1988 Games in Seoul.

Atlanta 1996

Gymnastics

GYMNASTICS MIGHT HAVE remained relegated to the far-back pages of Olympic Games history, with discontinued and unlamented sports like croquet and tug-of-war. Then, in 1972, along came a blonde, pig-tailed Byelarussian teenager

Olga Korbut (Munich, 1972)

named Olga Korbut to change all that. Korbut was just an alternate on the Soviet team going into the Munich Games. She got a chance to compete only when a teammate was injured; but it didn't take her long to capture the fancy of the world. Korbut opened with a brilliant routine in the uneven parallel bars, but a series of miscues the next day ended her chances for the all-around championship and left her in tears. She wasn't finished, however. She rebounded to win two gold medals and a silver in individual events.

Four years later, in Montreal, it was Romanian Nadia Comaneci's turn. Like Korbut, Comaneci was a diminutive 4-foot-11. But she was a very different gymnast. Olga was flash and style; Nadia was fearlessness and calm. During the team com-

petition, the fourteen-year-old Comaneci received the first perfect 10 score ever awarded in Olympic Games competition. Before the Games were over, she would reach perfection six more times. But she never relished the spotlight the way Korbut did.

Trent Dimas (Barcelona, 1992)

No U.S. woman had ever won an individual gymnastics medal in the Olympic Games until West Virginian Mary Lou Retton, a girl whose grin could illuminate any arena, arrived at the 1984 Games in Los Angeles, to test a field diluted by a Soviet bloc boycott. Retton, at 4 feet, 8 3/4 inches and 94 pounds, exuded power and athleticism. Despite the fact she had to have torn knee cartilage removed just six weeks before the competition, she earned perfect 10s in the floor exercise and vault and edged Romanian Kati Szabo for the all-around gold medal.

A footnote: Between 1956 and 1964, when gymnasts still labored in the shadows, Larissa Latynina of the Soviet Union won eighteen medals, more than any athlete in Olympic Games history.

In men's gymnastics, Japan and the Soviet Union have dominated recent competition, with Soviet Alexsandr Dityatin becoming the first male to receive a score of 10, in 1980. American Trent Dimas was a popular champion in 1992, taking a gold medal in the horizontal bar, while Vitaly Scherbo of the Unified Team won six gold medals in Barcelona, a record for gymnasts.

Men's Basketball

I T USED TO BE THE BIGGEST sure thing at the Olympic Games. The U.S. men would win the gold medal in basketball. From 1936, when competition began in Berlin, to the final at Munich in 1972, the Americans won sixty-two games without a loss. Most of the time, it wasn't even close. Then came that surreal, early-morning scene in Munich, when the U.S. rebounded from eight points down with six minutes to play to beat the Soviet Union, 50–49. Or so it seemed. All sorts of weird things began to happen, with just three seconds to play. The game seemingly ended a couple of times after that, with the U.S. ahead. But it didn't end officially. Then autocratic secretary-general R. William Jones of the International

Amateur Basketball Federation ordered the clock set back to three seconds, the Soviets sent a length-of-the-court pass to Alexsandr Belov, and he pushed over two U.S. defenders to score the winning basket. Officially. U.S. coach Hank Iba argued long and hard, but to no avail. The Americans filed a protest, but it was rejected, three votes to two, by a five-man Jury of Appeal.

U.S. vs. Czechoslovakia (Munich, 1972); Americans Brewer (11), Joyce (14), Burleson (at the rim)

The U.S. players were so upset that they voted unanimously not to accept their silver medals. The bad feelings remained for two decades, even though the Americans came back to win gold medals in 1976 and 1984, when their average margin of victory over outclassed opponents was 32 points a game.

Michael Jordan (Barcelona, 1992)

It wasn't until 1992 that some measure of closure seemed to be achieved, when the U.S. sent the "Dream Team"—a squad composed mostly of top professional players rather than the usual collegians—to Barcelona. Led by the likes of Magic Johnson, Michael Jordan, and Charles Barkley, the team's performance was absolutely dreamy. The average victory margin for the U.S. this time, over eight opponents, was 43.8 points. The gold medal game was a 117–85 wipeout of Croatia. At one point in the first half, the Americans actually trailed, 25–23, but Jordan, the top player for the U.S., said, "We weren't worried." The result proved that they didn't need to be. Somewhere, the late Hank Iba was smiling.

Other Highlights

THE MOUTH BEGAN ROARING at the 1960 Olympic Games in Rome. He was Cassius Marcellus Clay then, his conversion to Muhammad Ali years away. But the magic already was there in this eighteen-year-old from Louisville, and he enveloped all he surveyed, including five straight opponents in the light heavyweight division. Because of that performance, and the sheer force of his personality, he remains perhaps America's most memorable Olympic Games fighter ever.

Until a slump in recent years, the United States fared very well in Olympic Games boxing. Fidel LaBarba

Kristen Babb-Sprague (Barcelona, 1992)

won a gold medal (Paris, 1924), and so did Floyd Patterson, the two Sugar Rays, Seals and Leonard, Leon and Michael Spinks, Joe Frazier, and George Foreman, who lumbered around the ring with a tiny American flag in his hand after his super-heavyweight victory at Mexico City in 1968.

But other countries have done well, too. Super heavyweight Teofilo Stevenson of Cuba is the only man to win three gold medals in the same division. His height, his power (only twice in eleven Olympic Games bouts between 1972 and 1980 did opponents go the distance with him), and his continuing skill made him the scourge of Munich, Montreal, and Moscow.

Canada made a splash in the 1988 Olympic Games, when Carolyn Waldo was victorious in synchronized swimming, winning her nation's first gold medal of the Seoul Games. Waldo built such a big lead over American Tracie Ruiz-Conforto after the compulsory figures that she had no problem holding on for the victory. In 1992, Kristen Babb-Sprague, the wife of major league baseball player Ed Sprague, returned the favor for the U.S., edging Canadian Sylvie Frechette for the gold medal by 0.131 of a point.

In weightlifting, two very big men and a small one stand out. American Paul Anderson won a super heavyweight weightlifting gold medal in 1956, despite having to lose 60 pounds (to 303) before the Olympic Games to get in condition and then having to battle a strep throat during the competition. Mammoth Vasily Alexeyev of the Soviet Union, whose weight varied between 335 and 345 pounds, won super heavyweight golds in both Munich and Montreal, where his girth was the subject of continuing awe.

Bulgaria's Ivan Ivanov, who stood just over 5 feet tall and weighed only 114 pounds, won a 1992 flyweight division gold medal with a combined lift of 584 pounds.

Atlanta's Centennial Olympic Games Celebration

Atlanta Prepares for the Olympic Games . . . and Beyond

ON SEPTEMBER 18, 1990, the International Olympic Committee selected Atlanta as host for the 1996 Centennial Olympic Games. From that moment forward, the citizens of this progressive metropolis—from volunteers to business leaders—have joined hands in common cause. As the global spotlight focuses on their city, they are

Georgia State Capitol Building

hard at work preparing for the seventeen summer days when they will demonstrate Southern hospitality on a scale never before seen.

Many of these preparations are transforming the Atlanta landscape. Over $2 billion will be

spent to construct the sports facilities, homes and hotels, sidewalks, and parks that will accommodate the athletes and other visitors who come to the Games.

More important than the structures themselves are the spirit, foresight, and planning that have gone into them. The citizens of Atlanta have

Hockey venue, Morris Brown University

Rowing venue, Lake Lanier

Atlanta 1996

used the Olympic Games as a catalyst to make the city more prosperous and beautiful—in short, a better place to live.

Civic leaders look to the Olympic Games' building boom as a way to increase the already strong pace of economic development and investment. New hotels, new office buildings, and an increased airport capacity will improve a city that already is regarded as the communications, transportation, and financial capital of the South, as well as one of the top ten American cities in which to do business.

Revitalization of urban areas, including new housing, pedestrian walkways, and a beautiful Centennial Olympic Park, will provide building blocks for a more livable city center. In addition, public and private organizations are working to build or rehabilitate low-income housing in many neighborhoods.

Health enthusiasts of all kinds will find facilities to meet their needs. Those interested in the outdoor lifestyle will have a new network of paths across the metro area for jogging and bicycling. Baseball fans will take their seventh-inning stretch in a brand new stadium, while those seeking a more vigorous workout will have access to refurbished or new facilities for hockey, swimming, and tennis, just to name a few.

Olympic Stadium under construction

There's more, but you'll need to come to Atlanta to experience it all. When you do come, whether in the summer of 1996 or the spring of 2020, the legacy of the Olympic Games will be waiting for you.

1996 Atlanta Olympic Games Preview

THE CENTENNIAL OLYMPIC GAMES in Atlanta will be bigger than the 1992 Barcelona Games in many ways, none more so than when it comes to female athletes.

More than 3,700 women are expected to compete in the 1996 Games. That's approximately 700 more than the number who participated in Barcelona and the largest total ever in the Olympic Games.

Golfer Margaret Abbott, who in 1900 at Paris became the first U.S. woman to win a gold medal, no doubt would be astounded. Through much of Olympic Games history, female sports took a far-back seat to the men's events. For example, women's track and field wasn't added to the Games until 1928, when just five women's events were held. Individual women's gymnastics didn't join the roster until 1952. Women's basketball didn't arrive until 1976.

Women's softball is the only new sport for either gender on the Atlanta Olympic Games agenda, but women's soccer will join men's soccer for the first time. And there have been several women's disciplines added within the twenty-six sports, including the triple jump and 5,000 meters in track and field, beach volleyball, team synchronized swimming, individual and team épée competition in fencing, and mountain biking in cycling.

The attention surrounding women's basketball is such that the U.S., which hasn't fared too well in the sport internationally in recent years, hired a fulltime coach—Tara VanDerveer of Stanford—back in April of 1995. Part of the contract was that she had to take a year off from college coaching to devote full attention to the national team. Unlike her Olympic Games predecessors,

she'll have the benefit of being able to lead a squad into Atlanta that has worked as a unit for more than a year.

It's all according to plan—and a new way of thinking about women's athletics at the Olympic Games. When VanDerveer was hired, U.S.A. basketball chairman C. M. Newton said, "We pledge to you our total commitment as you lead us into this new era of women's basketball."

Tara VanDerveer

"Our goal is to win a gold medal in Atlanta," VanDerveer said. "There's no guarantee, but I think the new U.S. format gives us our best chance to do that."

The growth and innovation of the Games don't stop there.

"We'll have 271 medal events," said Dave Maggard, who finished fifth in the shot put at the 1968 Olympic Games and is director of sports for The Atlanta Committee for the Olympic Games. "That's almost 100 more than when I competed in Mexico City."

There will be about 11 million tickets to the 1996 events available for sale—"as large a number as Barcelona and the 1984 Olympic Games in Los Angeles combined," Maggard said.

He added that the scope and complexity of the Atlanta Olympic Games competition will dwarf that of the very successful L.A. Games, the last Olympic Games held in this country.

"Much more is being done with timing, scoring, and results," said Maggard, who was athletic director at California-Berkeley and the University of Miami before taking the Olympic Committee job. "These really will be the high-tech Games. And there are so many more venues than in L.A. The sports department is working with the venue people on $500 million worth of venues and designs."

The bulk of the competition will take place within the Olympic "ring," an imaginary circle with a radius of one and a half miles emanating from downtown Atlanta, and at Stone Mountain Park, sixteen miles from the Olympic Games Center. Soccer preliminaries will be held in Birmingham, Miami, Orlando, and Washington, D.C.; canoe-kayak events at Ocoee Whitewater Center in Cleveland, Tennessee.

A pre-Olympic-Games acclimation program for athletes from various countries has been set up at sites throughout the Southeast.

It's expected that the Summer Games will have a $5.1 billion impact on Georgia's economy between 1991 and 1997, the main portion of that in 1995 and 1996. "Everyone expects a tremendous transformation in a city that stages the Olympic Games," Maggard said. "That is happening in Atlanta, and changes will keep on occur-

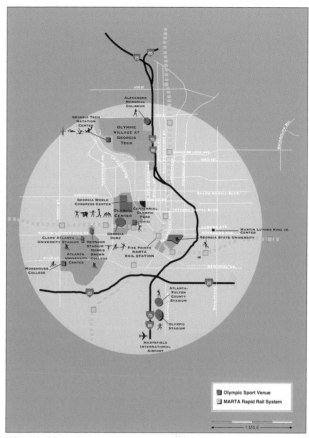

Olympic Ring venue map

ring. The Games will have a very significant impact on the whole region, too."

Maggard expects the Atlanta Olympic Games will serve as a beacon for top American athletes who want to compete for their country on U.S. soil. And he believes the 1996 Games may have a similar lure for the rest of the world.

"When the Olympic Games are held in the U.S.," he said, "everybody around the world thinks we have the capability of doing it better than anybody."

He's doing all he can to make sure that they're right.

OVERLEAF: *Jacques Pépin's "Cold Cream of Pea Soup with Mint," "Red Wine & Cassis Strawberries," and "Chicken Chasseur" (pages 55–57)*

PART II
THE RECIPES
· · · · · · · · · · · · ·

INTRODUCING AMERICA'S

*L*ike the athletes, they come from many lands— Europe, Asia, the Americas.

Marcel Desaulniers

Emily Luchetti

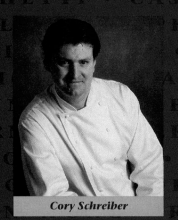

Cory Schreiber

They trained at state universities and prestigious culinary acade-mies, in the best kitchens of Europe, and at home under the watchful eyes of their parents.

Johnny Rivers

Fred Halpert

They come bearing the finest ingredients, innovative cooking techniques, and unique perspec-tives on food.

FINEST CHEFS AND COOKS

Together, they have created the melting pot that we call American cuisine.

Donna Nordin

Cassandra Mitchell

Michael Cordua

On the following pages, over fifty of America's finest chefs and cooks present some of their favorite recipes for you to enjoy at home. The chefs— and their recipes—are categorized by region, reflecting the area of the United States in which they currently reside.

The regions are presented in the following order: East, South, Midwest, Southwest, Northwest/Hawaii, and the West Coast. Within each region, chefs are presented in alphabetical order by last name.

See page 205 for Chef Index

See page 206 for Recipe Index

ANN AMERNICK

Ann Amernick, one of the most highly regarded pastry chefs and
authors in the United States, does private specialty pastry work
in Washington, D.C. She's been a pastry chef at many noted restaurants
in the area and was the assistant pastry chef at the White House
in 1980 and 1981.

Ann is the author of two cookbooks, including *Special Desserts*,
and was a 1992 nominee for Pastry Chef of the Year by the James Beard
Foundation. In 1994 she was named as one of the Ten Best
Pastry Chefs in America by *Chocolatier* magazine.

Miniature Gingersnaps

Chocolate Fantasy

MINIATURE GINGERSNAPS

. . . .

INGREDIENTS

³/4 *cup (1¹/2 sticks) unsalted
   butter, softened*

1 *cup packed dark brown sugar*

¹/4 *cup molasses*

1 *large egg*

2 *cups all-purpose flour*

1 *teaspoon baking soda*

2 *teaspoons ground ginger*

1¹/2 *teaspoons ground cinnamon*

¹/2 *teaspoon ground cloves*

PREPARATION

■ Heat oven to 350°F. Line three cookie sheets with parchment paper. Beat butter and brown sugar in a mixing bowl with electric beaters until light and fluffy. Add molasses and egg; mix just until combined.

■ Sift together flour, baking soda and spices; mix into butter mixture with a rubber spatula until thoroughly blended. Fit a pastry bag with a ¹/2-inch plain tip. Fill the pastry bag ²/3 full with dough and pipe mounds ¹/2 inch in diameter 2 inches apart on cookie sheets. Bake 10 to 12 minutes or until cookies feel dry and firm on top.

NOTE: May add 2 tablespoons chopped candied ginger to batter.

• ONE HUNDRED TINY COOKIES •

CHOCOLATE FANTASY

. . . .

INGREDIENTS

Cake

¹/₂	cup half-and-half
10	ounces semisweet chocolate, broken up
1	tablespoon rum
¹/₂	cup (1 stick) cold unsalted butter, cut into bits
5	large egg yolks
¹/₃	cup sugar, divided
5	large egg whites
¹/₂	cup cornstarch, sifted
³/₄	cup apricot preserves

Glaze

8	ounces semisweet chocolate
¹/₂	cup (1 stick) unsalted butter, softened

PREPARATION

- *To prepare the cake:* Heat oven to 350°F. Butter and flour two 8-inch round cake pans.

- Place a medium metal mixing bowl over hot but not boiling water. Add half-and-half, chocolate and rum to bowl; heat, stirring frequently until chocolate has melted. Remove bowl from the heat and add the butter bit by bit, beating with a whisk or hand-held electric mixer.

- In a separate bowl, beat egg yolks and 1 tablespoon of sugar until light and lemon-colored. Fold the egg yolk mixture into the chocolate mixture. In another bowl, beat the egg whites until they hold soft peaks, then gradually beat in the remaining sugar until the whites are stiff and glossy. Stir the cornstarch into the chocolate mixture until incorporated. Stir a quarter of the whites into the chocolate mixture to lighten the batter, then fold in the remaining whites.

- Scrape the batter into prepared pans and bake 20 minutes or until a few crumbs cling to a pick when inserted in the center. Cool the cakes in the pans for 10 minutes, then invert onto a cooling rack. When completely cool, place 1 cake layer on a plate and cover with apricot preserves. Top with the second layer, bottom side up.

- *To prepare the glaze and serve:* Combine the chocolate and butter in a small saucepan; heat over low heat, stirring frequently, until melted and smooth. Let mixture cool for a few minutes, then pour about a third of it over the top of the cake just to the edge.

- Cool the remaining glaze to room temperature by placing the pan in a bowl of ice water for a few minutes. With an electric mixer, beat the glaze until it is thick and fluffy; spread it around the side of the cake. Serve at room temperature and slice into slender wedges.

• EIGHT TO TEN SERVINGS •

DANIEL BOULUD

Daniel Boulud is one of the most highly recognized and brilliant chefs in New York City today. Raised in Lyons, France, on his family's farm, Daniel worked in the kitchens of some of the most prestigious chefs in Europe. After his tenure as executive chef at the world-renowned restaurant, Le Cirque, in New York, he opened his own restaurant, Daniel, in 1993. The restaurant received a four-star rating from the *New York Times* and was named one of the ten best restaurants in the world by the *International Herald Tribune*.

Daniel was voted Best Chef of the Year by his professional colleagues in the Chefs in America Association, and was honored by the James Beard Foundation as the 1992 Chef of the Year. His highly acclaimed cookbook *Cooking with Daniel Boulud* was published by Random House in 1993.

Summer Corn Risotto

Lemon-Herb Chicken Cooked Under a Brick

Fresh Fruits with Mint Cream

SUMMER CORN RISOTTO

. . . .

INGREDIENTS

6	*ounces bacon, sliced ¼ inch thick (about 7 slices)*
4	*cups chicken stock*
4	*ears corn, husks and silk removed*
3	*tablespoons unsalted butter, divided*
2	*cups sliced chanterelle mushrooms (about ½ pound)*
	salt and freshly ground pepper
1	*tablespoon minced chives, divided*
¼	*cup finely chopped green onions*
1½	*cups Italian arborio rice*
¼	*cup dry white wine*
2	*tablespoons grated Parmesan cheese*
4	*fresh sage leaves, chopped*

PREPARATION

■ Heat oven to 400°F. Place bacon on a baking sheet and cook until browned, about 10 minutes. Remove to paper towels to drain and cool. Chop the bacon into small pieces and set aside. Bring the chicken stock to a simmer in a medium saucepan.

■ In a large pot, boil the corn in salted water for 3 minutes; drain. Cut the kernels from the cob with a knife; set ¼ cup of kernels aside. In a food processor, purée the remainder with ¼ cup chicken stock; set aside.

■ Melt 1 tablespoon butter in a heavy sauté pan over high heat. Add the chanterelles and sauté, stirring frequently, until lightly browned. Season with salt and pepper. Stir in half the chives.

■ Melt another tablespoon of butter in a medium saucepan over medium heat. Add the green onions; cook 1 minute. Add the rice; cook and stir for about 3 minutes until well coated, but do not brown. Add the wine and cook 2 minutes. Slowly stir in the warm chicken stock to the level of the rice (about 1 cup) and simmer. Stir continually and add the rest of the chicken stock ½ cup at a time, as it is absorbed by the rice.

■ In 16 to 18 minutes when done, stir in the remaining butter, Parmesan cheese, corn purée, whole corn kernels, sage, half the bacon and half the mushrooms. Season with salt and pepper. Add more chicken stock if needed to moisten the risotto.

■ Serve the risotto in warm shallow bowls. Top with remaining bacon, mushrooms and chives.

• FOUR TO SIX SERVINGS •

Atlanta 1996

LEMON-HERB CHICKEN COOKED UNDER A BRICK

. . . .

INGREDIENTS

2	*free-range chickens, about 2½ pounds each*
4	*garlic cloves, peeled and quartered lengthwise*
3	*sprigs fresh thyme*
3	*sprigs fresh rosemary*
	salt
	crushed black peppercorns
3	*lemons*
6	*tablespoons olive oil, divided*
¼	*cup chives, cut into ½-inch lengths*

PREPARATION

- Split each chicken along the backbone and cut between the breasts to halve them; remove excess fat. Flatten halves on the skin side with a heavy skillet.

- Stud each breast and each leg with a few pieces of slivered garlic. Break up thyme and rosemary sprigs and stud each breast and leg with sprigs on inside of chicken. Season chickens with salt and pepper. Slice two lemons.

- In a large shallow dish, combine the chickens, lemon slices and 4 tablespoons of oil; cover and refrigerate 6 hours or overnight.

- Heat oven to 475°F.

- Heat 2 cast-iron skillets over high heat. Add 1 tablespoon olive oil to each skillet and place the chickens in the skillets, skin side down with lemon slices and herbs on top. Wrap 4 bricks in aluminum foil and place them atop the chicken halves to press them down in the skillet. Cook 8 to 10 minutes over medium-high heat until the skin is golden brown. Place the skillets in the oven and roast 20 minutes. Remove the bricks, turn the chickens over and cook 10 to 15 minutes, until tender.

- Remove the chickens to a platter. Halve the remaining lemon and squeeze the juice over the chicken. Scatter chives over the top.

• FOUR SERVINGS •

FRESH FRUITS WITH MINT CREAM

· ·

INGREDIENTS

Mint Cream

1	**cup heavy cream**
1	**cup milk**
1/3	**cup sugar, divided**
2	**bunches (about 4 ounces) fresh mint**
5	**egg yolks**
1	**cup water**
1	**tablespoon crème de menthe liqueur (optional)**

Fruits

4	**apricots, pitted, sliced**
2	**peaches, peeled, pitted, sliced**
1/4	**honeydew melon, pared, seeded, cut into thin slices**
1/2	**pint basket strawberries, hulled, cut into halves**
1/2	**pint basket raspberries**
1	**cup cherries, pitted, halved**
2	**kiwis, pared and sliced**
	juice of 1 lemon
2	**tablespoons sugar**
	leaves from 1 sprig fresh mint, chopped

PREPARATION

■ *To prepare the mint cream:* Stir together the cream, milk and half the sugar in a medium saucepan over medium-high heat. Bring mixture to a boil, stirring constantly. Strip the mint leaves from their branches; add 2/3 of the leaves to the cream mixture. Remove the pan from the heat, cover and let stand 5 minutes.

■ Meanwhile, whisk the egg yolks with the remaining sugar in a mixing bowl until foamy. Return the mint cream to the stove top, uncover, and bring back to a boil. Slowly pour the hot mint cream over the egg mixture, whisking constantly. Strain the custard back into the pan; discard the mint leaves.

■ Place the pan over low heat and cook, stirring constantly, until the mixture has thickened and almost reached the boiling point. Pour the cream into a bowl, stir for a few minutes and set aside to cool.

■ Bring 1 cup water to a boil in a small saucepan. Add the remaining mint leaves; boil 1 minute. Strain and discard the water. Add the blanched mint leaves, crème de menthe and cream mixture to the container of a blender or food processor. Process until smooth. Strain the mint cream into a bowl and refrigerate to chill.

■ *To prepare the fruits and assemble:* Mix the fruits in a bowl with lemon juice, sugar and mint; refrigerate to chill. Spoon the mint cream onto the bottom of a large, deep chilled dish and arrange the fruits on top.

· **FOUR TO SIX SERVINGS** ·

DANIEL BRUCE

Daniel Bruce is executive chef at the Boston Harbor Hotel,
a small luxury hotel in Boston, Massachusetts, which includes the
acclaimed Rowes Wharf Restaurant. Prior to joining the Boston Harbor
Hotel, Daniel worked at the 21 Club in New York City as executive chef,
the youngest in the history of the club.

Daniel was selected as the 1992 Chef of the Year for Boston by
Chefs in America and, in the same year, he was honored as one of the
Best Hotel Chefs in America by the James Beard Foundation. In 1993
Daniel was celebrated as a Distinguished Visiting Chef at Johnson
& Wales University, his alma mater—only the third alumnus to be
chosen in the fourteen-year history of the program. Renowned as the
chef of the Boston Wine Festival, Daniel pairs his stylized regional cuisine
with outstanding wines each year at the hotel.

*Sautéed New England Wild Mushrooms over
Stoneground Cornmeal Polenta*

*Mint Roasted Rack of Lamb with Ragout
of Harvest Vegetables*

*Vermont Mascarpone & Caramelized Apples in a
Crisp Cylinder with Cider Syrup*

SAUTEED NEW ENGLAND WILD MUSHROOMS OVER STONEGROUND CORNMEAL POLENTA

. . . .

INGREDIENTS

Sauce

5	cups chicken stock
1/2	cup heavy cream

Wild Mushrooms

2	tablespoons butter
2	shallots, thinly sliced
2	teaspoons minced garlic
2 1/2	cups sliced assorted wild mushrooms
	salt and pepper

Cornmeal Polenta

1/4	cup butter
1 1/2	cups milk
1/2	cup white cornmeal
1	tablespoon chopped mixed fresh herbs, such as parsley, rosemary and thyme
	salt and pepper

PREPARATION

■ *To prepare the sauce:* Bring chicken stock to a boil in a medium saucepan; continue to boil until reduced to 1 cup. Reduce heat and whisk in cream; simmer until sauce thickens slightly. Set aside.

■ *To prepare the mushrooms:* Heat a large heavy sauté pan over high heat. When hot, add butter followed by shallots, garlic and mushrooms. Sauté, stirring almost constantly until mushrooms are lightly browned. Season with salt and pepper.

■ *To prepare the polenta and assemble:* Combine butter and milk in a medium saucepan; heat to a simmer, stirring until butter melts. Slowly pour in cornmeal, whisking constantly to avoid lumps. Simmer 15 minutes over low heat, stirring occasionally. Stir in herbs; season to taste with salt and pepper.

■ Portion a spoonful of polenta on each of 5 small serving plates. Spoon mushrooms over polenta and ladle on sauce.

• FIVE SERVINGS •

MINT ROASTED RACK OF LAMB WITH RAGOUT OF HARVEST VEGETABLES

· · · · · · · · · · · · · · · · · · ·

INGREDIENTS

Harvest Vegetables

6	tablespoons butter
1	onion, thinly sliced
1	carrot, thinly sliced
½	cup thinly sliced rutabaga
2	small potatoes, cut into quarters (1 cup)
1	cup diced butternut squash
½	cup thinly sliced parsnip
1	cup chopped kale leaves
1	tablespoon minced thyme
	salt and pepper

Rack of Lamb

½	cup (1 stick) butter, softened
½	cup bread crumbs
½	cup chopped mint
1	egg yolk
¼	cup honey
	salt and pepper
2	Frenched 8-boned lamb racks (about 1¼ pounds each)
1½	cups dry red wine
1½	cups blueberries

PREPARATION

■ *To prepare the vegetables:* Melt butter over medium heat in a large heavy saucepan. Add onion; sauté until tender. Add carrot, rutabaga and potatoes; cook until partially cooked through. Add squash and parsnip; cover and cook until vegetables are tender. Add kale and thyme; cook until kale has wilted. Season with salt and pepper.

■ *To prepare the lamb and assemble:* Heat oven to 450°F. In a food processor, blend together butter, bread crumbs, mint, egg and honey; season to taste with salt and pepper.

■ In a large ovenproof sauté pan, sear lamb on both sides to brown. Place pan in oven and roast 11 minutes. Cool, 15 minutes or longer, then place butter mixture on top of each rack, spreading evenly. Return lamb to oven for 10 minutes for medium-rare. Remove racks from pan to a carving board and let rest 5 minutes. Pour off grease.

■ Add wine and blueberries to pan. Cook over high heat, scraping bottom of pan to loosen brown bits; boil to reduce sauce to 1½ cups. Strain sauce through a wire mesh sieve. Season with salt and pepper.

■ Portion vegetables onto serving plates. Slice racks and arrange 3 chops on each plate. Spoon sauce around lamb.

· FIVE SERVINGS ·

VERMONT MASCARPONE & CARAMELIZED APPLES IN A CRISP CYLINDER WITH CIDER SYRUP

INGREDIENTS

Crisp Cookie Cylinders

9	tablespoons butter
1	cup powdered sugar
2	egg whites
1	cup plus 2 tablespoons flour
	ground cinnamon

Caramelized Apples

7	tart green apples cored, quartered and sliced
$^{1}/_{4}$	cup butter
2	tablespoons sugar
1	teaspoon ground cinnamon
1	teaspoon ground nutmeg

Mascarpone Filling

4	egg yolks
$^{2}/_{3}$	cup sugar, divided
2	pounds mascarpone
2	tablespoons dark rum
3	cups heavy cream

Cider Syrup

$^{1}/_{2}$	gallon apple cider
	whole cranberries for garnish
1	cup sugar

PREPARATION

- *To prepare the cylinders:* Heat oven to 350°F. In a mixer bowl, beat butter and sugar until light and fluffy. Add egg whites and beat until blended. Mix in flour just until incorporated. Starting with a 5x7-inch rectangle of posterboard, cut out a 3x5-inch window in the center as template. Butter and flour a flat cookie sheet with no sides. Lay the template on the cookie sheet and spread the batter in the window $^{1}/_{16}$ to $^{1}/_{8}$ inch thick. Lift off the template. Repeat, making 1 or 2 rectangles per sheet. Sprinkle lightly with cinnamon.

- Bake 4 to 6 minutes until lightly browned. Remove the cookie sheet to a cooling rack. Working quickly, remove a rectangle with a spatula and form around a rolling pin to make a cylinder. Cool and then slip off the rolling pin. Repeat.

- *To prepare the caramelized apples:* Heat a heavy large sauté pan over high heat. Add apples, butter and sugar; sauté until golden brown. Remove pan from heat; stir in spices.

- *To prepare the mascarpone filling:* In a mixer bowl, beat egg yolks and $^{1}/_{3}$ cup sugar about 5 minutes. Mixture will triple in volume. In a second bowl, beat together mascarpone and rum until stiff. In another bowl, beat cream and remaining sugar until softly whipped. Fold all 3 mixtures together until smooth.

- *To prepare the cider syrup and assemble:* In a large saucepan, boil cider until reduced to about $1^{1}/_{2}$ cups. Lightly poach cranberries in 1 cup of water and 1 cup sugar. Drizzle cider syrup on dessert plates in zig-zag lines. Place a pastry cylinder upright in the center of each plate. Fill $^{1}/_{3}$ to the top with caramelized apples, and then with mascarpone filling. Top with a mint sprig. Place poached cranberries randomly on the plate.

• MAKES FOURTEEN •

Atlanta 1996

CHARLES CARROLL

Charles Carroll is executive chef of the Balsams Grand Resort Hotel,
a four-star, four-diamond resort located in Dixville Notch,
New Hampshire.

Charles is a 1986 graduate of the Culinary Institute of America.
He has received over fifty national and international awards, including
the American Culinary Federation President's Medallion in 1990.
Charles was selected as one of the Great Country Inn Chefs of 1993 by
the James Beard Foundation. He currently serves as Apprenticeship
Coordinator for one of the country's leading chef
apprenticeship programs.

Marinated Swordfish Steaks

Lemon-Lime Sauce for Fish

Steamed Boston Brown Bread with Raisins

MARINATED SWORDFISH STEAKS

· · · · · · · · · · · · · · · · · · ·

INGREDIENTS

¼	*cup dry white wine*
	pinch saffron threads
¾	*cup olive oil*
1	*tablespoon honey*
2	*teaspoons finely chopped parsley*
1	*teaspoon fresh lemon juice*
½	*teaspoon salt*
½	*teaspoon minced ginger*
½	*teaspoon minced garlic*
½	*teaspoon dried thyme leaves*
	pinch cayenne pepper
6	*swordfish steaks*

PREPARATION

■ Bring wine and saffron to a boil in a medium saucepan. Remove pan from heat and add olive oil, honey, parsley, lemon juice, salt, ginger, garlic, thyme and cayenne pepper. Allow marinade to cool completely.

■ Rinse swordfish steaks and pat dry. Place steaks in a glass baking dish; pour on marinade. Cover and refrigerate up to 6 hours.

■ Remove steaks from marinade and grill over charcoal or gas until fish turn from translucent to opaque throughout, 7 to 10 minutes. Turn steaks once during cooking.

· SIX SERVINGS ·

Atlanta 1996

LEMON-LIME SAUCE FOR FISH

INGREDIENTS

	juice and finely grated zest of 1 lime and 1/2 lemon
1/4	*cup Rose's lime juice*
1/4	*cup sugar*
2	*cups heavy cream*
8	*ounces (2 sticks) butter, at room temperature, cut into pats*

PREPARATION

■ Bring lime juice and zest, lemon juice and zest and Rose's lime juice to a boil in a medium saucepan. Boil until only 1 or 2 tablespoons of liquid remains. Add sugar and stir to dissolve. Add cream and boil until reduced to 1 cup.

■ Remove pan from heat and whisk in softened butter, piece by piece. Strain sauce through a wire mesh sieve.

• ABOUT TWO CUPS •

STEAMED BOSTON BROWN BREAD WITH RAISINS

INGREDIENTS

1	*cup yellow cornmeal*
1	*cup whole wheat flour*
1	*cup rye flour*
1	*teaspoon baking soda*
1	*teaspoon salt*
3/4	*cup molasses*
1 1/2	*cups buttermilk*
1	*cup raisins*

PREPARATION

■ Generously grease two 1-quart tin cans, such as coffee cans. Stir together the cornmeal, both flours, baking soda and salt in a mixing bowl. Add mixture of molasses and buttermilk; mix until smooth and well blended. Stir in raisins.

■ Scrape batter into cans, dividing evenly. Cover tops tightly with foil. Place cans in a pot large enough to hold the cans with 1 or 2 inch clearance all around. Fill the pot with hot water halfway up the sides of the cans.

■ Cover the pot and bring the water to a simmer; lower the heat and barely simmer for 2 hours or longer until a pick inserted in the center comes out clean. Cool the loaves on a wire rack until just warm before unmolding.

• TWO LOAVES •

Atlanta 1996

BOB KINKEAD

Housed in a Foggy Bottom row house in Northwest Washington, D.C.,
Bob Kinkead describes his restaurant, Kinkead's, as "an
American brasserie with a heavy emphasis on seafood." He adapts
unique dishes from around the world to American ingredients and tastes,
resulting in light, yet intense and full-flavored fare.

Bob has received considerable attention as a chef in the Washington
metropolitan area, including the 1992 *Washingtonian Magazine*
Restaurateur of the Year Award, the 1992 Chefs in
America Washington-Area Chef of the Year Award and the
1992 Restaurant Association of Metropolitan Washington
Chef of the Year Award.

Scandinavian Salmon Stew with Dill

Portuguese Roast Monkfish with Clams & Chorizo

Chocolate Crème Brûlée

Atlanta 1996

SCANDINAVIAN SALMON STEW WITH DILL

. . . .

INGREDIENTS

2	slices bacon, cut into ¼-inch pieces
1	small onion, diced
1	small leek, white part only, diced
3	shallots, minced
6	medium mushrooms, sliced
¾	pounds skinless salmon fillets, cut into 1-inch pieces
¼	cup dry white wine
2½	cups fish stock
2	medium potatoes, peeled, diced and blanched
1½	cups heavy cream
1	ear corn, kernels cut from the cob
	salt and pepper
2	tablespoons chopped fresh dill
2	tablespoons chopped fresh chives

PREPARATION

■ Heat a large heavy pot over medium heat; add the bacon and cook until crisp. Remove the bacon to drain on paper towels.

■ To the bacon fat in the pan add the onion, leek and shallots; sauté until the onion is transparent. Add the mushrooms and sauté about 4 minutes. Add the cubed salmon and sauté 4 minutes more. Remove the fish and vegetables and set aside.

■ Add the wine to the pot and cook, stirring until most of the wine has evaporated. Add the fish stock and potatoes; simmer until the potatoes are tender. Pour in the cream; season to taste with salt and pepper.

■ Bring the soup to a simmer; add the reserved fish and vegetables, the corn and the reserved bacon; simmer 2 to 3 minutes. Stir in the dill and chives.

• SIX SERVINGS •

PORTUGUESE ROAST MONKFISH
WITH CLAMS & CHORIZO

· · · · · · · · · · · · · · · · · · · ·

INGREDIENTS

¹/₄	*pound Portuguese chorizo sausage (about 2 sausages)*
12	*medium shrimp*
1¹/₂	*cups fish stock or bottled clam juice*
1¹/₂	*cups chicken stock*
¹/₂	*cup dry white wine*
30	*littleneck clams, scrubbed clean*
2	*pounds skinless monkfish*
	salt and pepper
4	*tablespoons olive oil, divided*
1	*medium onion, diced*
5	*garlic cloves, minced*
³/₄	*cup peeled, seeded and finely diced tomato*
	juice and finely grated zest of 1 lemon
¹/₄	*cup finely chopped Italian parsley*
4	*green onions, chopped*
2	*anchovies, finely chopped*
2	*teaspoons capers*

PREPARATION

■ Bring water to a boil in a medium saucepan over high heat, add the chorizo, reduce the heat and simmer 7 to 8 minutes to cook through. Drain. When the chorizo is cool enough to handle, remove the casing and cut into ¹/₂-inch pieces; set aside.

■ Peel and devein shrimp; cut each into 4 or 5 pieces and set aside.

■ In a medium saucepan, bring the fish stock, chicken stock and white wine to a boil. Add the clams to the stock and cook 4 to 5 minutes, just until they open. Remove the clams and set aside. Boil the stock in the pan until reduced by ¹/₃. Strain and set aside.

■ Cut the monkfish into 6 equal portions; season with salt and pepper. Heat 1 tablespoon of olive oil in a large heavy sauté pan over high heat. Add 3 pieces of monkfish and brown quickly on both sides. Transfer fish to a baking sheet. Repeat with another tablespoon of oil and remaining fish.

■ Heat oven to 400°F.

■ In a large heavy sauté pan, heat remaining 2 tablespoons olive oil over medium heat. Add the onion and sauté 3 minutes. Add the chopped garlic and cook until the onion is transparent. Stir in the tomato, chorizo, shrimp and reduced stock; cook until the shrimp firms up and turns pink. Stir in the lemon juice, zest, parsley, green onions, anchovies and capers. Add the clams and cook to heat through.

■ Meanwhile, bake the fish 5 to 10 minutes until it turns from translucent to opaque throughout. Let stand 3 minutes and then slice each portion into 5 pieces. Spoon the sauce mixture onto each of 6 warm plates. Place the monkfish on top.

· SIX SERVINGS ·

Atlanta 1996

CHOCOLATE CREME BRULEE

· · · · · · · · · · · · · · · ·

INGREDIENTS

1½	*cups heavy cream*
1	*cup milk*
6	*ounces bittersweet or semisweet chocolate*
6	*large egg yolks*
½	*cup granulated sugar*
½	*cup dark brown sugar*

PREPARATION

- Heat oven to 325°F. In a small heavy saucepan, heat cream and milk over medium-low heat just until bubbly. Remove from heat; add chocolate and stir until melted.

- In a medium mixing bowl, combine eggs yolks and granulated sugar. Beat with a wire whisk just until combined. Slowly whisk the chocolate cream into the egg mixture.

- Place 8 small ovenproof ramekins in a baking pan. Set the baking pan on oven rack. Pour custard mixture evenly into dishes. Pour very hot water into the baking pan around the dishes, about halfway up the sizes.

- Bake 18 to 24 minutes or until a knife inserted near the center comes out clean. Remove dishes from the water bath; let cool on a wire rack. Cover and chill for at least 2 hours or overnight.

- Before serving, remove custards from refrigerator; let stand 15 minutes. Heat a broiler. Sprinkle brown sugar on top of custards and place them under the broiler just until the sugar caramelizes. Serve immediately.

· EIGHT SERVINGS ·

JEAN-LOUIS PALLADIN

Jean-Louis Palladin was born and raised in the Gascony town of Condom, France, by parents of Spanish and Italian heritage. He credits his mother with introducing him to the world of food and teaching him the fundamentals of classical cooking. Today, Jean-Louis is considered a world-class chef, trained in the finest kitchens of Europe.

In 1979 Jean-Louis came to Washington, D.C., to open Jean-Louis at the Watergate Hotel, a small, intimate restaurant located in the heart of the District, adjacent to the Kennedy Center for the Performing Arts. The fixed-price menu changes daily and is handwritten by the chef himself.

Jean-Louis has received numerous accolades, and many of his creations have been recorded in his book *Jean-Louis: Cooking with the Seasons*.

Brandade of Cod

*Tagine of Lamb with Dried Apricots &
Orange Flower Water*

Tarte au Chocolat

BRANDADE OF COD

. . . .

INGREDIENTS

Brandade

1	pound salt cod
	milk
1	cup olive oil
6	garlic cloves, crushed
1	pound russet potatoes, pared, cut into large chunks
	salt and pepper

Tempura Mix

$^1/_2$	cup bread flour
$^1/_2$	cup cake flour
2	teaspoons baking powder
$^1/_2$	teaspoon salt
1	cup water
	oil for frying

PREPARATION

■ *To prepare the brandade:* Place cod in a large bowl; cover with cold water. Refrigerate for 2 days, changing water 4 times. Rinse soaked cod; place in a large saucepan. Cover with milk; bring to a boil. Reduce heat; simmer about 10 minutes until fish is done. Drain and flake fish, discarding bones and skin.

■ Meanwhile, heat 1 cup olive oil with garlic; set aside to cool and let the oil infuse with garlic. Remove garlic.

■ Boil potatoes in salted water until tender. Mash potatoes with enough olive oil to make them smooth. In a food processor, process the salt cod until evenly chopped. With the machine running, gradually pour in oil until the mixture is smooth and spreadable. Combine the mashed potatoes and salt cod mixture. Season to taste with salt and pepper.

■ *To prepare the tempura mix and deep-fry:* In a mixing bowl, stir together flours, baking powder and salt. Gradually stir in water.

■ In a deep fryer or heavy saucepan, heat oil to 365°F. Dip small portions of potato and cod mixture in tempura batter to completely coat; let excess batter drip back into bowl. Carefully lower pieces into hot oil, cooking several at a time without crowding. Deep-fry 1 to 3 minutes, turning occasionally until lightly browned and crisp. Drain on paper towels.

NOTE: At the restaurant, Jean-Louis serves the brandade as an appetizer set on small portions of edible seaweed.

• EIGHT SERVINGS •

TAGINE OF LAMB WITH DRIED APRICOTS & ORANGE FLOWER WATER

INGREDIENTS

1	*tablespoon curry powder*
2	*tablespoons ras el hanout**
1	*teaspoon ground coriander*
4	*tablespoons olive oil, divided*
3	*pounds lamb shoulder, cut into chunks*
2	*onions, thinly sliced*
3	*cups lamb consommé or beef stock*
1	*cup water*
1/8	*teaspoon crumbled saffron threads*
1	*cup chopped dried apricots*
1	*cup diced turnips*
1	*cup each sliced yellow squash and zucchini*
	salt and pepper
1	*tablespoon or more orange flower water**
	cooked couscous or basmati rice

* Ingredients are available in markets that sell Middle-Eastern ingredients.

PREPARATION

■ Stir together the curry powder, ras el hanout, coriander and 2 tablespoons olive oil in large mixing bowl. Add the lamb and turn well to coat. Cover and marinate in the refrigerator 2 hours or overnight.

■ Heat remaining 2 tablespoons olive oil in a heavy flameproof casserole or pot over medium-high heat. Lightly brown the lamb in batches in the oil. Return all the lamb to the casserole and add the onions; cook, stirring 5 minutes. Add the consommé, water and saffron.

■ Bring to a boil, reduce the heat, cover and simmer for 1 hour. Stir in the dried apricots and turnips; simmer another 30 minutes. Add the squash the last 5 to 10 minutes of cooking. Season to taste with salt and pepper. Add the orange flower water, adjusting the flavor to suit your taste.

■ Serve the tagine in wide shallow bowls over couscous or rice.

• FIVE TO SIX SERVINGS •

TARTE AU CHOCOLAT

. . . .

INGREDIENTS

³/₄	*cup heavy cream*
¹/₃	*cup milk*
8	*ounces bittersweet chocolate, chopped*
1	*egg, slightly beaten*
	baked 9-inch tart shell

PREPARATION

- Heat oven to 350°F.

- Heat the cream and milk in a heavy medium saucepan until very hot. Remove from the heat; add the chocolate and stir until melted.

- Cool the mixture 5 minutes; beat in the egg. Pour the chocolate into a baked tart shell.

- Bake 20 to 30 minutes until the filling is set. Cool on a wire rack before cutting.

• EIGHT SERVINGS •

JACQUES PEPIN

Jacques Pépin, master chef, author and teacher, was born in
Bourg-en-Bresse, France. He grew up in his parents' restaurant and began
his formal apprenticeship at the Brand Hotel de l'Europe
in his hometown.

For the past twenty years, Pépin has devoted his time to writing,
consulting and teaching. He writes columns for the *New York Times* and
Food & Wine magazine, and has written many best-selling cookbooks.
His top-rated cooking show, "Today's Gourmet with Jacques Pépin,"
has aired on PBS since 1991.

Jacques is Dean of Studies at the French Culinary Institute in
New York City and teaches a graduate course, "Culture and Cuisine,"
at Boston University. He is a founder of the American Institute of Wine
and Food, and is member of the board of trustees for the
James Beard Foundation.

Cold Cream of Pea Soup with Mint

Chicken Chasseur

Red Wine & Cassis Strawberries

COLD CREAM OF PEA SOUP WITH MINT

. . . .

INGREDIENTS

1	*tablespoon virgin olive oil*
1	*medium onion (about 5 ounces), peeled and thinly sliced (1¼ cups)*
3	*cups chicken stock, preferably homemade unsalted and defatted or lower-salt canned chicken broth*
¾	*teaspoon salt (less if canned broth is used)*
1	*cup (loose) fresh mint leaves*
1	*package (10 ounces) frozen petite peas, unthawed, or equivalent amount of fresh peas*
1½	*cups plain yogurt, regular or nonfat*
1	*tablespoon unsalted butter*
1	*teaspoon sugar*
¼	*teaspoon Tabasco hot pepper sauce*

PREPARATION

■ Heat the oil until hot in a large stainless steel saucepan. Add the onion, and sauté for 2 minutes. Stir in the stock and salt, and bring the mixture to a boil over high heat.

■ After reserving a few of the mint leaves to decorate the finished soup, add the remainder along with the peas to the boiling stock. Bring the mixture back to a boil (this will take 3 or 4 minutes), and continue to boil it vigorously over high heat for 3 minutes.

■ Immediately place half the pea mixture in the bowl of a food processor, and process it until very smooth. Transfer the purée to a bowl, and process the remaining pea mixture along with 1 cup of the yogurt and the butter. Strain both batches of the purée through a fine strainer for a smooth soup. (If not strained, the soup will have a slightly granular texture.) Mix in the sugar and Tabasco, cover with plastic wrap, and refrigerate until serving time.

■ At serving time, process the remaining yogurt for a few seconds, until it is liquefied (it should have the consistency of a salad dressing). Divide the soup among four bowls, and swirl 1 to 2 tablespoons of the liquefied yogurt over each serving. Decorate with reserved mint leaves, and serve.

NOTE: This soup is bright green when freshly made. If you are preparing it more than a few hours ahead, do not add the yogurt until just before serving, because the acid in it will tend to discolor the peas, making the soup a darker, less appealing shade. It is important that you use thin-skinned fresh peas or frozen petite peas here for a smooth result.

• FOUR SERVINGS •

Atlanta 1996

CHICKEN CHASSEUR

. . . .

INGREDIENTS

1	tablespoon virgin olive oil
8	skinless chicken thighs, with all surrounding fat removed (about 2 pounds)
1	small leek (5 ounces), trimmed, cleaned, and coarsely chopped (1³⁄₄ cups)
1	medium onion (4 ounces), peeled and chopped (1 cup)
1¹⁄₂	tablespoons all-purpose flour
1	cup dry white wine
1	can (15 ounces) whole peeled tomatoes in juice
5	cloves garlic, peeled, crushed, and finely chopped (1 tablespoon)
20	medium mushrooms (about 12 ounces)
1	teaspoon chopped fresh thyme
1	teaspoon chopped fresh rosemary
1	teaspoon salt
¹⁄₂	teaspoon freshly ground black pepper
1	tablespoon soy sauce
1	tablespoon chopped fresh tarragon

PREPARATION

■ Heat the olive oil until it is hot in a large nonstick skillet. Add the chicken thighs in one layer, and cook them for 5 minutes on each side over medium to high heat. Transfer the thighs to a large, sturdy saucepan, arranging them side by side in a single layer in the pan.

■ To the drippings in the skillet add the leek and onion, and sauté for 30 seconds. Add the flour, mix it in well, and cook for about 30 seconds. Then mix in the wine and tomatoes. Bring the mixture to a boil over medium heat, and pour it into the saucepan containing the chicken. Stir in the garlic, mushrooms, thyme, rosemary, salt, pepper, and soy sauce.

■ Bring the mixture to a boil over high heat, stirring occasionally to prevent the chicken from scorching, then cover the pan, reduce the heat to low, and cook for 25 minutes. Sprinkle on the tarragon, and mix it in. Serve two thighs per person with some of the vegetables and surrounding liquid.

NOTE: In the original versions of this dish, unskinned chicken pieces were browned in a great amount of butter. Although the skin was crisp initially from the browning, it would soften and become gummy by the time the other ingredients were added and the dish cooked as a stew. I use skinless chicken thighs in my flavorful update of this dish. After sautéeing the thighs in a little olive oil, I finish them in a chasseur sauce containing onions and leeks and flavored in the traditional manner with white wine, tomatoes, and mushrooms. This dish can be prepared up to a day ahead; if you do so, however, cook it initially for 15 minutes instead of 25. The chicken will continue to cook a little in the hot sauce as it cools and again as the dish is reheated later, so it will be cooked properly by serving time.

• FOUR SERVINGS •

Atlanta 1996

RED WINE & CASSIS STRAWBERRIES

INGREDIENTS

3	*cups ripe strawberries, washed and hulled*
3	*tablespoons sugar*
3	*tablespoons cassis (black currant-flavored liqueur) or crème de mûres (blackberry-flavored liqueur)*
3/4	*cup dry, fruity red wine*
1	*tablespoon shredded peppermint leaves*
4	*tablespoons sour cream (optional)*
	cookies (optional)

PREPARATION

■ Quarter the berries, and place them in a bowl with the sugar, liqueur, wine, and mint. Mix well, and serve immediately, or refrigerate (for up to 8 hours) until serving time.

■ Spoon the berries and marinade into wine goblets for serving. If desired, top each dessert with a dollop of sour cream, and serve it with a cookie.

NOTE: In wine-growing regions, berries—particularly strawberries—are typically combined with the wine from that area, and sometimes a liqueur, and served as a dessert. Here, I mix strawberries with a fruity red wine and black currant or blackberry liqueur and serve them in the classic way, spooned into wine goblets. If desired, top the desserts with a little sour cream, and serve them with cookies.

• FOUR SERVINGS •

THOMAS VACCARO

Thomas Vaccaro was the executive pastry chef at the famous
Waldorf Astoria Hotel in New York City, where he oversaw
the preparation of all baked goods—pastries for three restaurants,
room service and grand ballroom events. He is now pastry chef of Trump
Plaza in Atlantic City. Trained at the Culinary Institute of America in
Hyde Park, New York, Thomas has received accolades in many
culinary competitions throughout his career.

*Angel Food Cake & Frozen Yogurt with
Strawberry-Rhubarb Syrup*

Chocolate Beignets with Sour Cream Dipping Sauce

*Chocolate Banana Decadence with Mixed Berries
& Champagne Sabayon*

ANGEL FOOD CAKE & FROZEN YOGURT WITH STRAWBERRY-RHUBARB SYRUP

· · · · · · · · · · · · · · · · ·

INGREDIENTS

3	**cups sliced rhubarb with tops and bottoms removed**
2	**pint-size baskets strawberries, hulled, sliced**
2	**cups water**
3/4	**cup sugar**
1/2	**cup Riesling wine**
1	**teaspoon minced fresh ginger**
1	**cinnamon stick**
1/2	**vanilla bean, split**
	zest of 1 orange
1/2	**bunch fresh mint**
	angel food cake
	low-fat frozen yogurt or vanilla ice cream

PREPARATION

■ Combine rhubarb, strawberries, water, sugar, wine, ginger, cinnamon, vanilla bean and orange zest in a large heavy saucepan over medium heat. Simmer 15 minutes, stirring occasionally.

■ Reserve a few mint leaves for garnish; coarsely chop remaining leaves and add to pan. Remove pan from heat and let mixture stand 15 minutes, then strain through a wire mesh sieve, retaining the syrup. Cool syrup to room temperature.

■ At serving, spoon a pool of syrup onto each of 6 dessert plates. Place a slice of angel food cake in the center of each plate and a scoop of frozen yogurt on the cake. Garnish with reserved mint.

· SIX SERVINGS ·

Atlanta 1996

CHOCOLATE BEIGNETS WITH SOUR CREAM DIPPING SAUCE

INGREDIENTS

3½	cups all-purpose flour
2	cups sugar
6	ounces (1½ cups) unsweetened cocoa powder
1	tablespoon baking powder
1½	teaspoons salt
7	eggs
2	cups milk
⅓	cup vegetable oil
3	ounces semisweet chocolate, melted
	oil for frying
	powdered sugar

Sour Cream Dipping Sauce

2	cups sour cream
1	cup sugar
2	tablespoons Grand Marnier liqueur

PREPARATION

- In a large mixing bowl, combine the flour, sugar, cocoa powder, baking powder and salt; stir to thoroughly blend. In a separate bowl, whisk together eggs, milk and oil. Make a well in the center of the dry ingredients and pour the egg mixture into the well; mix just to incorporate. Stir in melted chocolate just until blended. Refrigerate the batter for 2 hours to firm up.

- In a deep-fryer or heavy saucepan, heat oil to 350°F. With a small ice cream scoop or a spoon, carefully drop a few scoops of batter into hot oil. Deep-fry 2 to 3 minutes, turning several times in the oil; the outside will be cooked and crisp but the center will be the consistency of thick melted chocolate. Drain on paper towels. Repeat with remaining batter.

- Dust beignets with powdered sugar and serve with sour cream dipping sauce.

- *To prepare the sour cream dipping sauce:* Stir together sour cream, sugar and Grand Marnier liqueur.

• MAKES THIRTY-SIX BEIGNETS •

CHOCOLATE BANANA DECADENCE WITH MIXED BERRIES & CHAMPAGNE SABAYON

INGREDIENTS

Chocolate Banana Decadence

1	cup (2 sticks) unsalted butter
8	ounces semisweet chocolate, coarsely chopped
4	eggs
1/2	cup sugar
1/4	cup Godiva chocolate liqueur
1	banana, thinly sliced

Champagne Sabayon

6	large egg yolks
1/3	cup sugar
1/3	cup Champagne or sparkling wine

Berries

2	cups sliced strawberries or any combination of small whole berries, such as raspberries, boysenberries or blueberries

PREPARATION

■ *To prepare the chocolate banana decadence:* Heat oven to 350°F. Melt butter and chocolate in a small heavy saucepan over low heat; remove from heat and stir until smooth.

■ In a large bowl with electric beaters, lightly beat eggs. Continue beating, slowly adding sugar. Add melted chocolate and liqueur; mix until blended.

■ Butter six 6-ounce soufflé dishes. Spoon batter into dishes, filling about 1/3 full. Top with sliced bananas. Spoon on remaining batter. Bake 12 minutes; desserts will still be molten in the center. Remove to wire racks to cool.

■ *To prepare the champagne sabayon:* Combine the egg yolks and sugar in a medium-size bowl. Whisk well until pale yellow. Add the Champagne in a slow stream, whisking constantly until the sabayon is frothy and has doubled in volume.

■ *To assemble:* Unmold chocolate decadence onto dessert plates. Surround with berries. Spoon warm sabayon over the berries.

• SIX SERVINGS •

ELLA & DICK BRENNAN

Ella Brennan and brother Dick Brennan started in the restaurant business as teenagers, and today run the Commander's Palace Family of Restaurants with siblings John, Dottie, and children. Commander's Palace in New Orleans is their flagship restaurant; they also run six more restaurants in New Orleans and the Houston area.

The Brennans and Commander's Palace have received many awards, including the Travel/Holiday Fine Dining Award, the Mobil Four Star Dining Award, Playboy Critic's Choice Award, Food Arts Silver Spoon Award, the DiRoNA Award, and Best Restaurant, James Beard Foundation.

Eggs Sardou

Shrimp & Fettuccine

Chocolate Molten Soufflé

Atlanta 1996

EGGS SARDOU

· · · · · · · · · · · · · · · · · · ·

INGREDIENTS

2	*pounds fresh spinach*
2	*cups water*
1¹/₂	*tablespoons unsalted butter*
¹/₄	*cup finely chopped green onions*
1	*cup béchamel sauce (medium white sauce)*
¹/₂	*teaspoon salt*
¹/₄	*teaspoon freshly ground black pepper*
8	*artichoke bottoms, cooked (fresh or canned)*
8	*eggs, poached*
2	*cups hollandaise sauce*

PREPARATION

■ Wash spinach thoroughly and discard thick heavy stems. In a medium saucepan, bring water to a rapid boil; add spinach and cook until wilted and barely tender. Plunge spinach into ice water to stop the cooking; drain, pat dry with paper towels. The spinach should be very dry.

■ Melt butter in a large sauté pan. Add green onions and sauté, stirring for 2 minutes. Add spinach and sauté for 2 minutes longer. Stir in béchamel sauce; season with salt and pepper. Set aside and keep warm.

■ Place ¹/₄ of the creamed spinach on each of 4 warmed plates and top with 2 warm artichoke bottoms. Put 2 poached eggs on the artichoke bottoms and spoon on ¹/₂ cup hollandaise sauce. Serve immediately.

· FOUR SERVINGS ·

SHRIMP & FETTUCCINE

INGREDIENTS

24   medium shrimp, peeled and
        deveined, shells reserved
        for broth

$1/2$ cup (1 stick) unsalted butter,
        softened, divided

2   garlic cloves, minced

4   teaspoons finely chopped
        parsley

$1/2$ onion, chopped

4   fresh mushrooms, sliced

$1/4$ cup peeled, seeded and finely
        chopped tomato

$1/2$ cup chopped green onions

2   teaspoons Creole seafood
        seasoning

2   cups cooked fettuccine noodles

$1/2$ cup dry white wine

PREPARATION

■ Place shrimp shells in a medium saucepan and cover with water. Bring to a boil; lower heat and simmer 15 minutes. Strain broth and return to saucepan. Boil broth until reduced to $1/4$ cup. Set aside.

■ Melt half the butter in a large saucepan over medium heat. Add the garlic, parsley, onion, mushrooms, tomato, green onions and seafood seasoning; sauté 2 to 3 minutes. Add the broth, cooked fettuccine, shrimp and wine; cook over medium high heat until liquid is almost evaporated. Remove pan from heat, add remaining butter and stir gently until butter is melted and sauce creamy. Serve immediately.

• FOUR SERVINGS •

CHOCOLATE MOLTEN SOUFFLE

. . . .

INGREDIENTS

White Chocolate Sauce

1	*cup heavy cream*
1/4	*cup sugar*
1	*cup chopped white chocolate*
2	*tablespoons light rum*

Chocolate Soufflé

5	*eggs*
1	*cup sugar*
1/4	*cup butter, softened*
1	*cup sifted cake flour*
18	*ounces bittersweet chocolate, melted*
	powdered sugar and fresh raspberries, for garnish

PREPARATION

■ *To prepare the white chocolate sauce:* Combine cream and sugar in a small saucepan; bring to a boil. Remove pan from heat; stir in white chocolate until smooth, then add rum. Set aside.

■ *To prepare the chocolate soufflé and assemble:* Heat oven to 400°F. In a food processor, combine eggs and sugar until blended. Add butter; process 30 seconds. Add flour; process until smooth. Add chocolate; process until just incorporated. Liberally butter 6 individual soufflé cups; divide batter among cups. Bake 10 to 15 minutes. Cake should be cooked on the outside but still molten inside.

■ Spoon a pool of white chocolate sauce on each of 6 dessert plates. Unmold soufflé cakes onto plates and dust with powdered sugar. Garnish with fresh raspberries.

• SIX SERVINGS •

RICARDO DELEON

Ricardo DeLeon inherited a love for cooking from his parents,
both excellent cooks. After graduating from Johnson & Wales University
he cooked in hotels before joining Azalea as a sauté cook. Two years
later he was promoted to chef.

Azalea, located in the Buckhead district of Atlanta, Georgia,
is known for its fusion cuisine, an eclectic but skillful blending of
Hispanic, Asian and Mediterranean flavors. Ricardo, true to his heritage,
has developed many of the restaurant's signature dishes with a
characteristic Mexican style.

Chilled Tomato Soup with Cilantro Sour Cream

Azalea Burrito

Ice Cream Fresh Fruit Tostada

CHILLED TOMATO SOUP WITH CILANTRO SOUR CREAM

INGREDIENTS

7	**medium tomatoes**
1	**tablespoon olive oil**
1	**white onion, chopped**
1	**jalapeño pepper, finely chopped**
1	**head garlic, peeled, cloves cut in half**
4	**cups chicken stock**
1/2	**cup tomato paste**
1	**bunch cilantro**
1	**tablespoon ground cumin**
	salt and pepper to taste

Cilantro Sour Cream

1/2	**cup sour cream**
1	**teaspoon brown sugar**
1/4	**bunch cilantro, chopped**

PREPARATION

■ Heat oven to 400°F. Place tomatoes on a baking sheet and roast 20 to 30 minutes until they are soft and start to brown in spots. Remove from oven and allow tomatoes to cool; coarsely chop, reserving juices.

■ Heat oil in a large saucepan over medium-low heat. Add onion, jalapeño pepper and garlic; cook 15 to 20 minutes until soft. Add tomatoes with their juices, chicken stock and tomato paste. Tie up a bunch of cilantro with string and add to saucepan. Cover and cook 30 minutes over medium heat.

■ Remove cilantro and process ingredients in batches in a blender. Transfer soup to a large bowl. Stir in cumin and salt and pepper to taste. Refrigerate to chill. Serve soup cold topped with cilantro sour cream.

■ *To prepare cilantro sour cream:* Combine sour cream, brown sugar and chopped cilantro.

• FOUR TO SIX SERVINGS •

AZALEA BURRITO

INGREDIENTS

2	pounds venison or lean beef
1/4	cup vegetable oil, divided
2	medium onions
8	garlic cloves
3	cups dry red wine
1/2	cup packed brown sugar
1/2	cup chopped cilantro
2	teaspoons ground cumin
1	cup finely grated asiago cheese
1	cup chopped tomatoes
8	(8-inch) flour tortillas

PREPARATION

■ Cut venison into thin narrow strips. Heat 2 tablespoons oil in a large sauté pan over medium-high heat. Add venison in batches and brown lightly; remove and set aside.

■ Heat remaining oil in pan; add onions and garlic; sauté until onions become very soft. Add red wine and brown sugar; bring mixture to a boil and boil until reduced by about 3/4. Remove pan from heat; stir in cilantro, cumin, cheese, chopped tomatoes and venison. Season to taste with salt and pepper. Divide mixture among 8 tortillas and roll up like a burrito.

• EIGHT BURRITOS •

ICE CREAM FRESH FRUIT TOSTADA

INGREDIENTS

1/2	cup sugar
1	teaspoon ground cinnamon
	oil for frying
4	corn tortillas
1	quart favorite ice cream
2	kiwifruit, pared, sliced
7	strawberries, hulled and sliced
1	cup blueberries or blackberries
	chocolate sauce

PREPARATION

■ Combine sugar and cinnamon in a small bowl; stir to blend. Heat 1 inch of oil in a sauté pan over high heat. Deep-fry tortillas, 1 at a time in hot oil until crisp. Remove to paper towels and sprinkle with cinnamon-sugar mixture.

■ Place tostadas on 4 plates. Center a scoop or two of ice cream on tostadas. Arrange fruit on top and drizzle with chocolate sauce.

• FOUR SERVINGS •

Atlanta 1996

MARCEL DESAULNIERS

Marcel Desaulniers is executive chef and co-owner of the
Trellis Restaurant in Williamsburg, Virginia. A graduate of Culinary
Institute of America, Marcel has received a number of national awards,
including *Food & Wine* magazines's Honor Roll of American Chefs,
Who's Who of Cooking in America by *Cook*'s magazine, the Ivy Award from
Restaurants and Institutions, and the Silver Plate Award from the
International Foodservice Manufacturers Association.

Marcel has written four books: *The Trellis Cookbook, Death by Chocolate,
The Burger Meisters* and *Desserts to Die For*. In 1988 he was inducted
into the American Academy of Chefs, and he is a member of the Board
of Trustees for the Culinary Institute of America.

Oven-Roasted Vegetable Chowder

*Pan-Seared Chicken Breasts with Shrimp, Broccoli,
Country Ham & Toasted Peanut Butter*

Mocha Java Sorbet

OVEN-ROASTED VEGETABLE CHOWDER

. . . .

INGREDIENTS

3	*medium plum tomatoes*
	salt and pepper
½	*pound round red potatoes*
1	*large carrot*
1	*medium parsnip*
1	*medium turnip*
1	*tablespoon safflower oil*
1	*cup diced celery*
1	*cup diced onion*
4	*cups vegetable stock*
2	*tablespoons chopped fresh parsley*

PREPARATION

■ Heat oven to 200°F. Cut tomatoes into halves lengthwise, then into thirds lengthwise. Place skin-side down on a baking sheet lined with parchment paper. Season lightly with salt and pepper. Slowly roast the tomatoes for 3 hours. Remove from oven and cool to room temperature. Cut into ½-inch pieces.

■ Increase oven to 375°F. Cut potatoes into ½-inch cubes; place on a nonstick baking sheet. Season with salt and pepper. Roast 1 hour and 15 minutes until well browned, stirring with a spatula every 15 minutes or so. Remove from oven and cool to room temperature.

■ While the potatoes roast, pare the carrot, parsnip and turnip; cut into ½-inch cubes. Place on a nonstick baking sheet and season with salt and pepper. Roast 1 hour until lightly browned. Remove from oven and set aside until needed.

■ Heat oil in a 3-quart saucepan over medium heat. Add the celery and onion; sauté 5 minutes. Season with salt and pepper. Add the stock, roasted potatoes and roasted vegetables; bring to a simmer. Remove soup from heat and add roasted tomatoes and chopped parsley. Season with salt and pepper.

NOTE: The vegetables can be roasted a day or two in advance of making the chowder; store, tightly covered, in the refrigerator. For best flavor, prepare the soup 24 hours before serving; this will allow the flavor to develop fully.

• FOUR SERVINGS •

Atlanta 1996

PAN-SEARED CHICKEN BREASTS WITH SHRIMP, BROCCOLI, COUNTRY HAM & TOASTED PEANUT BUTTER

INGREDIENTS

1/2	**cup unsalted shelled peanuts**
1/2	**cup (1 stick) unsalted butter, softened**
	salt and pepper
4	**(4-ounce) boneless, skinless chicken breasts**
1	**tablespoon olive oil**
1 1/4	**pounds large shrimp, peeled, deveined and halved lengthwise**
1/4	**pound country ham, cut into strips 1 1/2 inches long and 1/8 inch wide**
2	**pounds broccoli, trimmed and cut into florets**

PREPARATION

■ Heat oven to 300°F. Place peanuts on a baking sheet and roast 20 minutes until golden brown. Remove from oven and allow to cool. When cool, finely chop 1/2 cup; reserve remaining peanuts for garnish. Combine chopped peanuts with softened butter. Season with salt and pepper; set aside. Reduce oven temperature to 200°F.

■ Place chicken breasts between parchment or waxed paper and uniformly flatten each breast with a meat cleaver or the bottom of a sauté pan. Lightly season chicken with salt and pepper. Heat a nonstick sauté pan over medium-high heat. Add chicken and sear 1 1/2 to 2 minutes per side until lightly browned. Transfer breasts to a nonstick baking sheet; baste with 4 tablespoons peanut butter and hold in oven while completing recipe.

■ Heat olive oil in a large nonstick sauté pan over medium-high heat. Add shrimp and ham; sauté 3 to 4 minutes. Season with salt and pepper.

■ Cook the broccoli in boiling salted water until tender but still crunchy; drain. Arrange the broccoli florets in a ring, stem ends toward the center, along the outer edge of 4 plates. Place a chicken breast in the center of each ring. Spoon shrimp and ham around breasts. Top each breast with a tablespoon of peanut butter and sprinkle with reserved toasted peanuts.

• FOUR SERVINGS •

MOCHA JAVA SORBET

· · · · · · · · · · · · · · · · · · ·

INGREDIENTS

1½	*cups strong brewed coffee*
2	*cups water*
2	*cups sugar*
6	*ounces unsweetened chocolate, chopped*
2	*ounces semisweet chocolate, chopped*
1	*teaspoon vanilla extract*

PREPARATION

■ Bring the coffee, water and sugar to a boil in a large saucepan over medium-high heat; stir until the sugar is dissolved. Place both chocolates in a bowl and pour about 1 cup hot liquid over the chocolate. Let stand 5 minutes. Whisk vigorously until mixture is very smooth, about 3 minutes. (If the mixture is not smooth, the sorbet will be grainy.) Add the remaining hot liquid and whisk until smooth.

■ Place the bowl in large bowl of ice and whisk while the mixture cools to a temperature between 40 and 45°F. Whisk in the vanilla.

■ Freeze mocha mixture in an ice cream maker following manufacturer's directions. Transfer sorbet to a freezer container, cover, and freeze for several hours before serving. Serve within 2 days.

· TWO QUARTS ·

Atlanta 1996

JONATHAN EISMANN

Jonathan Eismann cooks Asian-influenced American food
with a French head. It is this blending of flavors and techniques, which
has become known as Pacific Rim cuisine, that has put Jonathan's
restaurant, Pacific Time of Miami Beach, on the map. Pacific Time has
been heralded as one of America's Best New Restaurants
by both *Bon Appétit* and *Esquire* magazines. And the *Miami Herald*
gave Pacific Time its highest rating.

Jonathan was trained at the Culinary Institute of America
and has worked in the kitchens of some of the hottest and best
restaurants in the country. Currently he consults with restaurants, writes,
and constantly experiments with new flavors and recipes.

Pacific Time Pâte Imperiale

Napa Kim Chee

*Broiled Pink Florida Grapefruit with
Wild Flower Honey*

PACIFIC TIME PATE IMPERIALE

INGREDIENTS

$^3/_4$	cup rice vinegar
$1^1/_2$	teaspoons minced ginger
$1^1/_4$	teaspoons Japanese seven pepper spice*, divided
$1^1/_2$	teaspoons salt, divided
1	medium cucumber, pared, finely diced
1	quart water
$^1/_4$	cup lemon juice
6	medium shrimp, peeled and deveined
6	(9-inch) circles rice paper*
30	baby Romaine lettuce leaves, washed and dried, or large Romaine leaves torn into 2-inch pieces
12	fresh mint leaves

Dipping Sauce

$^1/_2$	cup rice vinegar
$^1/_2$	cup water
1	tablespoon finely chopped cilantro

* Ingredients are available in markets that
sell Asian foods.

PREPARATION

- Combine rice vinegar, ginger, $^1/_4$ teaspoon Japanese seven pepper spice and $^1/_2$ teaspoon salt in a bowl. Add cucumber and allow to marinate while preparing recipe.

- Bring 1 quart of water to a boil in a medium saucepan with remaining 1 teaspoon salt, lemon juice and remaining 1 teaspoon Japanese seven pepper spice. Add shrimp, reduce heat and simmer until shrimp firm up and turn pink. Drain and cool shrimp. Cut each shrimp lengthwise into 4 even slices.

- Soak rice paper in water for a few seconds; remove from water and place between damp cloths for several minutes until soft.

- Place 3 baby Romaine leaves on the center of each piece of rice paper. Top with sliced shrimp and marinated cucumber. Arrange 2 mint leaves on top and cover with 2 more Romaine leaves. Roll up rice paper. Serve with dipping sauce.

- *To prepare the dipping sauce:* Combine rice vinegar, water and cilantro in a bowl.

• SIX SERVINGS •

Atlanta 1996

NAPA KIM CHEE

INGREDIENTS

1	*cup rice wine vinegar*
½	*cup honey*
1	*teaspoon salt or to taste*
½	*teaspoon Japanese seven pepper spice*
½	*bunch cilantro, finely chopped*
1	*head Napa cabbage, shredded*

PREPARATION

■ Combine vinegar, honey, salt, Japanese seven pepper spice and cilantro in a mixing bowl; stir until thoroughly blended.

■ Add cabbage and marinate for 30 minutes to 1 hour (no more than 1 hour). Drain.

• ABOUT THREE CUPS •

BROILED PINK FLORIDA GRAPEFRUIT WITH WILD FLOWER HONEY

INGREDIENTS

24	*sections from large pink Florida grapefruit, cut away from the membranes*
1	*tablespoon sugar*
¼	*cup wild flower honey or other honey*

PREPARATION

■ Preheat broiler. Arrange grapefruit in one layer in a baking dish. Sprinkle with sugar and drizzle with honey.

■ Broil until hot and browned in spots.

• FOUR SERVINGS •

JOHN FOLSE

Chef John Folse is an authority on Cajun and Creole cooking
and culture, a national television cooking show host,
and the owner of two award-winning restaurants in South Louisiana:
Lafitte's Landing Restaurant in Donaldsonville, and White Oak
Plantation in Baton Rouge. He is also the owner of Louisiana's
Premier Products, a food manufacturing company specializing in soups,
sauces, entrées, meats and vegetables for foodservice distribution.

John is the recipient of numerous culinary awards and honors,
and has been recognized by local, state and international governments
for his continuing efforts to showcase America's regional
cooking around the world. In 1994 Chef Folse assumed the national
presidency of the American Culinary Federation, the largest association
of professional chefs in America.

Louisiana Seafood Gumbo

Chicken & Sausage Jambalaya

Bread Pudding Cake

LOUISIANA SEAFOOD GUMBO

INGREDIENTS

½	cup vegetable oil
¾	cup all-purpose flour
1	cup chopped onions
½	cup chopped celery
½	cup chopped green bell pepper
2	tablespoons chopped garlic
¼	pound andouille sausage, sliced
½	pound claw crab meat
6	cups shellfish stock or 3 cups bottled clam juice plus 3 cups water
1	cup sliced green onions
¼	cup chopped parsley
	salt to taste
	cayenne pepper to taste
	dash Louisiana Gold Pepper Sauce
½	pound shrimp, peeled and deveined
½	pound lump crab meat
12	shucked oysters
	cooked rice

PREPARATION

■ Heat oil in a large heavy pot over medium-high heat. Add flour and using a wire whisk, stir constantly until roux turns a rich golden brown color. Be careful to not let the roux scorch and burn.

■ Reduce the heat and add the onions, celery, bell pepper and garlic; cook, stirring 3 to 5 minutes until the vegetables are wilted. Add sausage; cook an additional 2 to 3 minutes. Stir in the claw crab meat, then slowly add the shellfish stock 1 cup at a time, stirring constantly until all is incorporated.

■ Bring to a boil, reduce heat and simmer gently 30 minutes. Add green onions and parsley; season to taste with salt, cayenne pepper and Louisiana Gold Pepper Sauce. Stir in shrimp, lump crab meat and oysters. Return to a simmer and cook 5 minutes. Serve gumbo over cooked rice.

• SIX SERVINGS •

CHICKEN & SAUSAGE JAMBALAYA

. . . .

INGREDIENTS

¹/₄	cup vegetable oil
2	pounds boneless fresh chicken, cubed
1	pound andouille sausage, sliced
2	cups chopped onions
2	cups chopped celery
1	cup chopped green bell pepper
¹/₄	cup chopped garlic
7	cups beef stock
2	cups sliced mushrooms
1	cup sliced green onions
¹/₂	cup chopped parsley
	salt and cracked black pepper
	dash of Louisiana Gold Pepper Sauce
4	cups long grain rice

PREPARATION

- In a large flameproof casserole or heavy pot, heat oil over medium-high heat. Add chicken and cook, stirring occasionally until chicken is dark brown on all sides. (It is important that the meat is well browned because the color of the jambalaya comes from the meat.)

- Add the sausage and cook 10 to 15 minutes more. Pour off all but a few tablespoons of fat. Add onions, celery, bell pepper and garlic; cook until vegetables are well browned. Add the beef stock and bring to a boil. Reduce the heat and simmer 15 minutes.

- Add mushrooms, green onions and parsley. Season to taste with salt, black pepper and Louisiana Gold Pepper Sauce. Add rice, reduce heat to low, cover casserole and cook 30 minutes. Remove casserole from burner and let stand 10 minutes. Adjust seasonings to taste.

• SIX SERVINGS •

Atlanta 1996

BREAD PUDDING CAKE

. . . .

INGREDIENTS

Bread Pudding

6	large eggs
4	cups milk
1	cup sugar
1/4	cup vanilla extract
1	tablespoon ground cinnamon
1	tablespoon ground nutmeg
1	tablespoon vegetable oil
1	loaf (10 ounces) French bread, sliced
1	cup raisins
1	cup chopped pecans

Praline Sabayon

3/4	cup dry white wine
1/2	cup praline liqueur
3	egg yolks
1/4	cup sugar

PREPARATION

■ *To prepare the bread pudding:* Whisk eggs in a mixing bowl until lightly beaten. Whisk in milk, sugar, vanilla, cinnamon, nutmeg and oil; mix until well blended.

■ Butter a 3-inch deep, 10-inch diameter layer cake pan or 1½ quart-casserole and place a layer of sliced bread into the pan, making sure there are no open spaces. Sprinkle on ⅓ of the raisins and pecans. Pour about ⅓ of the custard mixture on top. Continue layering until all the ingredients are used. (Use all custard during the preparation of this recipe. Do not discard.) Cover and refrigerate several hours or overnight.

■ Heat oven to 375°F. Place the cake pan in a larger baking pan on oven rack. Fill the larger pan with hot water to come 1 inch up the side of the cake pan. Bake about an hour until a knife inserted in the center comes out clean. Cool on a wire rack while preparing praline sabayon.

■ *To prepare the praline sabayon and serve:* Heat the wine and praline liqueur in a small saucepan. Combine the egg yolks and sugar in a mixing bowl, whisking well until pale yellow and creamy, about 3 minutes.

■ Combine the egg and wine mixtures in the top of a double boiler and cook over boiling water, whisking constantly until the sabayon is frothy and doubles in volume. Remove from the heat and continue to whisk 1 or 2 minutes. Serve with bread pudding.

• SIX TO EIGHT SERVINGS •

DONNA MCCABE

In 1973, Donna and her husband Charles bought the
Loveless Motel and Cafe, located near Nashville, Tennessee. It was then,
as it is now, a white clapboard farm house converted to a country-style
cafe with banks of "tourist court" motel rooms to the right and left.
Over time, the menu has remained much the same—delicious Southern
fried chicken, country ham and red-eye gravy, true Southern scratch
biscuits, and homemade peach and blackberry preserves.

The Loveless was selected as one of the five best places for
breakfast in America by CBS "This Morning" show, and has been featured
in countless magazine and newspaper articles. Today, son George
operates the business with his mother, while Donna greets customers and
maintains the Loveless's high standard of Southern hospitality.

Blackberry Preserves

Slow-Cooked Country Ham

Chess Squares

BLACKBERRY PRESERVES

. . . .

INGREDIENTS

| 10 | pounds fresh blackberries |
| 5 | pounds granulated sugar |

PREPARATION

- Remove any stems from blackberries and place in the bottom of a large pot. Add the sugar and bring slowly to a boil, stirring occasionally until the sugar dissolves.

- Cook until the mixture is thick and jam-like, stirring frequently as it thickens to prevent sticking. Ladle into clean, hot canning jars leaving $^{1}/_{2}$ inch headspace; seal. Process in a boiling water bath 15 minutes.

• ABOUT EIGHT PINTS •

SLOW-COOKED COUNTRY HAM

. . . .

INGREDIENTS

14	to 16 pounds country ham*
1	tablespoon ground allspice
1	teaspoon ground cloves
2	bay leaves
1	jar (16 ounces) sorghum molasses*

* Country hams and sorghum molasses can be ordered from Loveless Hams and Jams, 1-800-889-2432.

PREPARATION

- Remove the ham hock with a saw; save for soups and seasoning vegetables. Place the ham in a large pot and cover with water. Bundle up the spices and bay leaves in a square of triple-layered cheesecloth; tie with a string. Add the spice packet and molasses to the pot. Bring the liquid to a boil and boil for 5 minutes per pound of ham (1 hour and 10 to 20 minutes). Reduce the heat, cover the pot and simmer gently for 20 minutes per pound of ham ($4^{1}/_{2}$ to $5^{1}/_{2}$ hours).

- Remove the pot from the heat and let the ham cool in its cooking liquid until it is cool enough to handle. Remove the ham from the pot and trim off any fat. Carefully remove the ham bone. Refrigerate the ham before slicing thinly (it is easier to slice when cold). Serve the ham cold or reheat it if desired.

• ABOUT THIRTY-FIVE SERVINGS •

CHESS SQUARES

. . . .

INGREDIENTS

Crust

6	*tablespoons butter, softened*
$^1/_3$	*cup powdered sugar*
$1^1/_3$	*cups all-purpose flour*

Filling

$^1/_2$	*cup butter, softened*
$1^1/_2$	*cups sugar*
1	*tablespoon yellow cornmeal*
1	*tablespoon vanilla extract*
1	*tablespoon distilled white vinegar*
3	*eggs*

PREPARATION

■ *To prepare the crust:* Heat oven to 350°F. Beat butter in an electric mixer until soft and fluffy. Beat in sugar, then flour until crumbly.

■ Press dough into the bottom of a 9-inch square baking pan. Bake 20 minutes.

■ *To prepare the filling and bake:* Beat butter and sugar in an electric mixer until light and fluffy. Mix in cornmeal, vanilla, vinegar and eggs until thoroughly blended. Pour over crust.

■ Return to oven and bake 20 to 25 minutes until filling is nearly set. Cool on a wire rack and then cut into squares.

• SIXTEEN SQUARES •

LOUIS OSTEEN

Louis Osteen, chef/creator of Louis's Charleston Grill, was born in
Anderson, South Carolina, the son and grandson of theatre owners.
In 1975, he left the traditional livelihood of his ancestors to
pursue his passion for cooking and the regional foods of the South.
In 1980 he and his wife, Marlene, moved to Pawleys Island,
South Carolina, to open the Pawleys Island Inn. Immediately
Louis became a leader in defining a contemporary indiginous
American cuisine.

In 1989, Louis's desire to reach a larger audience combined with
the interest of the owners of the Omni Hotel at Charleston Place to
reformat their existing restaurant. In October 1989 Louis's
Charleston Grill opened to immediate praise and was selected by
Esquire magazine as one of the country's top twenty-five new restaurants.

Louis has received numerous honors and awards, including the
Restaurants and Institutions magazine Ivy Award; *Nation's Restaurant News*
Fine Dining Hall of Fame; the DiRoNA, awarded by Distinguished
Restaurants of North America, and the National Institute of Hospitality
Studies Great American Chef Award.

Brown Oyster Stew with Sesame Seeds

Oven-Roasted Catfish with Sweet Onion Marmalade

Fried Green Tomatoes

BROWN OYSTER STEW WITH SESAME SEEDS

INGREDIENTS

¹/₄	cup sesame seeds
2	tablespoons peanut oil
2	tablespoons finely diced pancetta
2	tablespoons finely chopped red onion
2	teaspoons all-purpose flour
24	oysters, shucked with their liquor strained and reserved
1³/₄	cups fish stock or bottled clam juice
2	small sprigs fresh thyme, leaves stripped from the branch
1¹/₄	cups heavy cream
2	tablespoons finely chopped fresh chervil or parsley
	salt and pepper
	oyster crackers or buttered toast fingers

PREPARATION

■ Place the seeds in a small heavy-bottomed sauté pan and toast over medium heat until they're browned and fragrant. Divide the seeds in half; roughly crush half the seeds. Set aside.

■ Pour oil into a large heavy-bottomed saucepan and place over medium heat. Add the pancetta and sauté lightly until crisp and lightly browned. Remove the pancetta to drain on paper towels.

■ Add the onion and crushed sesame seeds; sauté until the onion is lightly browned. Add the flour and cook, stirring another 2 minutes. Add the oyster liquor (reserved from shucked oysters), fish stock and thyme leaves; whisk over medium-high heat until the mixture simmers.

■ Meanwhile, warm the cream in a small saucepan and add to the mixture; simmer 5 minutes. Add the oysters, the remaining sesame seeds, pancetta and chopped parsley. Cook until the oysters just begin to curl. Remove from heat; season with salt and pepper. Divide the stew among 4 warmed bowls. Serve with oyster crackers or buttered toast fingers.

• FOUR TO SIX SERVINGS •

OVEN-ROASTED CATFISH WITH SWEET ONION MARMALADE

. . . .

INGREDIENTS

2	*pounds (3 to 4) sweet yellow onions, sliced crosswise and separated into rings*
2	*cups chicken stock*
1/2	*teaspoon fresh thyme leaves*
1	*cup heavy whipping cream*
2	*tablespoons balsamic vinegar*
	salt and pepper
8	*skinless catfish fillets, about 3 ounces each*

PREPARATION

■ Place the onions and chicken stock in a heavy-bottomed saucepan; cover and cook over medium heat 15 minutes. Remove the cover, add the thyme leaves and simmer over medium-high heat until most of the liquid evaporates and the onions start to lightly brown, stirring frequently toward the end of cooking.

■ Add the cream and cook until the mixture thickens. Add the vinegar and cook 2 minutes longer, then season to taste with salt and pepper. Remove the pan from the heat and set aside.

■ Heat oven to 350°F. Season the catfish fillets with salt and pepper. Lay the fillets skinned side up on a flat surface. Place 1 tablespoon of onion marmalade on each fillet. Beginning at the small tail end, roll the fillet into a tight spiral; secure with a wooden pick. Place the spirals about 1 inch apart in a buttered baking dish; top each with a tablespoon of onion marmalade.

■ Bake about 10 minutes until fillets are cooked through; remove from oven and let stand several minutes. Divide remaining sauce among each of 4 warmed plates. Remove wooden picks and place 2 fillets on each plate.

• FOUR SERVINGS •

Atlanta 1996

FRIED GREEN TOMATOES

· · · · · · · · · · · · · · · · · · ·

INGREDIENTS

6	*green tomatoes*
3	*cups buttermilk*
2	*tablespoons hot pepper sauce, such as Tabasco*
1	*cup yellow cornmeal*
1	*cup all-purpose flour*
1/2	*teaspoon baking soda*
1	*teaspoon salt*
1	*teaspoon freshly ground pepper*
	oil for frying or rendered bacon fat

PREPARATION

■ Cut tomatoes into 1/2-inch-thick slices. Combine buttermilk and hot pepper sauce in a wide shallow bowl; add tomatoes and let stand about 1 hour.

■ In a separate wide shallow dish, combine the cornmeal, flour, baking soda, salt and pepper. Drain the tomato slices and turn in flour mixture to coat. Place on a baking sheet and refrigerate 30 minutes for the coating to dry.

■ Heat 1/2 inch oil in a cast-iron frying pan. Carefully place as many tomatoes as will fit into the pan without overcrowding. Fry over medium-high heat turning once until browned. Remove to a baking sheet lined with paper towels and keep warm until serving. Repeat with remaining tomatoes. Keep warm until serving.

• FOUR TO SIX SERVINGS •

REIMUND PITZ

A native of Germany, Reimund Pitz immigrated to the
United States in a European apprenticeship program to attend the Disney
School of Culinary Arts. Shortly thereafter, he joined Disney and
progressed through the ranks. In 1988 he was promoted to executive
chef at Disney-MGM Studios.

Reimund is a recipient of the 1992 National Chef of the Year
Award given by the American Culinary Federation. In 1992 he was the
youngest chef to be inducted into The Honorable Order of
the Golden Toque, which recognizes only 100 of the top culinary
professionals in the United States.

Butter Lettuce Salad

Breast of Chicken Chardonnay

Butterscotch Bread Pudding

BUTTER LETTUCE SALAD

INGREDIENTS

2	**heads butter lettuce**
2	**plum tomatoes, finely diced**
2	**tablespoons lemon juice**
1	**tablespoon apple cider vinegar**
1/3	**cup olive oil**
	salt and pepper

PREPARATION

■ Cut heads of lettuce in half. Gently rinse lettuce in a bowl of ice water; drain in a colander. With a small piece of core attached to the lettuce, place a half, cut side up, on each of 4 salad plates. Sprinkle with tomatoes.

■ Whisk together lemon juice, vinegar and oil; season with salt and pepper. Drizzle dressing over salads.

• FOUR SERVINGS •

BREAST OF CHICKEN CHARDONNAY

INGREDIENTS

8	**boneless skin-on chicken breasts**
	salt and pepper
	all-purpose flour
3	**tablespoons clarified butter**
1 1/2	**cups sliced mushrooms**
1	**cup California Chardonnay**
1/2	**cup chicken stock**
1/2	**cup heavy cream**
1	**tablespoon whole mustard seeds**
1 1/2	**cups sliced leeks, blanched**

PREPARATION

■ Heat oven to 375°F. Season chicken breasts with salt and pepper; turn in flour to lightly coat. Heat 1 1/2 tablespoons clarified butter in a large heavy sauté pan over medium-high heat. Add 4 chicken breasts and brown on both sides. Repeat with more clarified butter and remaining chicken. Remove to a baking sheet; place in oven and bake about 15 to 20 minutes until chicken is tender.

■ Meanwhile, add mushrooms to the sauté pan and cook, stirring frequently, until they start to brown. Add wine and chicken stock; cook, stirring constantly, for several minutes. Add cream and mustard seeds; bring mixture to a boil and cook until reduced by almost half to a sauce-like consistency. Add leeks to sauce. Serve sauce over chicken breasts.

• FOUR SERVINGS •

Atlanta 1996

BUTTERSCOTCH BREAD PUDDING

INGREDIENTS

2	cups *1/2-inch cubes white bread*
1*1/4*	*cups half-and-half*
1	*tablespoon unsalted butter*
1/2	*teaspoon salt*
1/2	*teaspoon vanilla extract*
1/4	*cup packed dark brown sugar*
1	*large egg*
1	*large egg yolk*
	vanilla ice cream

PREPARATION

■ Heat oven to 350°F. Butter four 1¼-cup soufflé dishes or ramekins and divide bread cubes between them. Heat half-and-half, butter, salt and vanilla in a medium saucepan over medium heat; stir until butter has melted.

■ In a mixing bowl with a wire whisk, whisk together brown sugar, egg and egg yolk. Add hot mixture in a slow steady stream, whisking constantly. Pour custard over bread cubes, dividing evenly. Bake until puffed and golden brown, about 30 minutes. Serve warm with ice cream.

• FOUR SERVINGS •

JOHNNY RIVERS

Johnny Rivers, executive chef of Walt Disney World, joined
the Disney team in 1970 and subsequently helped open each Disney hotel
and theme park, including Euro-Disney in France. Johnny received
the Cornell Culinarian Hospitality Artist Award in 1989 and the National
Chefs Professional Award, sponsored by the L. J. Minor Corporation
and the American Culinary Federation, in 1994. In 1991 he was inducted
into Gourmet Services Chefs Hall of Fame. *Restaurant Hospitality*
magazine has rated him one of the ten most creative chefs in America.

Johnny has twice co-chaired summits for South Africa, raising
funds for the Tour for Hunger organization. In 1994, he co-authored
Down Home Healthy, published by the National Cancer Institute.
Most recently, he was the recipient of an honorary degree, Doctor of
Culinary Arts, from Johnson & Wales University.

Crab Cakes Boca

Catfish Stew & Rice

Peach Cobbler

CRAB CAKES BOCA

. . . .

INGREDIENTS

1	tablespoon butter
1/2	cup minced onion
1/2	cup minced celery
1	pound crab meat
1/2	cup bread crumbs
3	large eggs
1/2	cup mayonnaise
1	teaspoon all-purpose flour
1	tablespoon Dijon mustard
1	tablespoon finely chopped parsley
2	teaspoons Old Bay seasoning
1/2	teaspoon Worcestershire sauce
1/4	teaspoon cayenne pepper
1/4	teaspoon hot pepper sauce
1/2	teaspoon cracked black pepper
1/4	teaspoon salt
2	tablespoons each oil and butter for sautéeing
	lemon wedges

PREPARATION

- Melt butter in a small saucepan over medium heat. Add the onion and celery; sauté 3 to 5 minutes until onion is translucent.

- In a mixing bowl, combine crab meat, sautéed vegetables, bread crumbs, eggs, mayonnaise, flour, mustard, parsley, Old Bay seasoning, Worcestershire sauce, cayenne pepper, pepper sauce, black pepper and salt. Shape mixture into 8 patties.

- Heat 1 tablespoon each oil and butter in a large sauté pan; add 4 patties and brown on both sides. Repeat with remaining oil, butter and crab meat patties. Serve with lemon wedges.

• FOUR SERVINGS •

CATFISH STEW & RICE

INGREDIENTS

Hot 'n' Spicy Seasoning

1/4	cup paprika
2	tablespoons dried crushed oregano
2	teaspoons chili powder
1	teaspoon garlic powder
1	teaspoon ground black pepper
1/2	teaspoon cayenne pepper
1/2	teaspoon dry mustard

Catfish Stew

2	medium potatoes, pared and quartered
1	can (14 1/2 ounces) whole peeled tomatoes, undrained, tomatoes broken up
1	cup chopped onion
1	cup bottled clam juice
1	cup water
2	garlic cloves, minced
1/2	head green cabbage, coarsely chopped
1	pound catfish fillets
2	cups hot cooked rice
2	green onions, sliced

PREPARATION

■ *To prepare the hot 'n' spicy seasoning:* Combine paprika, dried crushed oregano, chili powder, garlic powder, ground black pepper, cayenne pepper and dry mustard.

■ *To prepare the catfish stew and serve:* In a large pot, combine potatoes, tomatoes and juice, onion, clam juice, water and garlic. Bring mixture to a boil, reduce the heat, and cook, covered, over medium-low heat for 10 minutes. Add cabbage; continue to cook 5 to 8 minutes, stirring occasionally.

■ Cut catfish fillets into 2-inch pieces; coat lightly with hot 'n' spicy seasoning. Add fish to pot; simmer for 5 minutes or until fish is cooked through. Scoop rice into 4 shallow soup bowls. Ladle soup over rice. Scatter green onions on top.

• FOUR SERVINGS •

Atlanta 1996

PEACH COBBLER

. . . .

INGREDIENTS

2¼	cups sliced peaches
½	cup sugar
2	teaspoons apricot brandy
2	tablespoons unsalted butter
2	teaspoons lemon juice
2	teaspoons vanilla extract
1	teaspoon ground cinnamon
¼	teaspoon nutmeg
1	tablespoon cornstarch dissolved in 2 tablespoons cold water
	dough for a 9-inch pie crust

PREPARATION

■ Heat oven to 325°F. Combine peaches, sugar, brandy, butter, lemon juice, vanilla, cinnamon and nutmeg in a medium heavy saucepan and bring to a boil over medium-high heat. Stir cornstarch mixture into peaches and cook until mixture thickens. Spoon peaches into 4 ovenproof bowls.

■ Roll out pie dough and cut into circles about 2 inches larger in diameter than the diameter of the ovenproof bowls. Place dough over bowls and crimp pastry to the rim. Cut 3 small steam vents on top. Bake 20 to 25 minutes until golden brown.

• FOUR SERVINGS •

GREG & MARY SONNIER

Greg and Mary Sonnier are among the growing number of successful restaurant chef couples. Both have training as professional cooks and started their cooking careers at Paul Prudhomme's famed K-Paul's in New Orleans. Together they opened Gabrielle Restaurant in New Orleans in March of 1992.

Gabrielle Restaurant has been recognized among the top ten restaurants by *The Times Picayune*, and has been featured in *Travel & Leisure*, *Gourmet* and *Food & Wine* magazines. In 1994 *Food & Wine* magazine named Greg among the Top Ten Chefs in America.

*Creole Crab Cakes
with Red Horseradish Sauce*

Crawfish Enchilada with Sauce Con Queso

CREOLE CRAB CAKES WITH RED HORSERADISH SAUCE

INGREDIENTS

4	teaspoons butter
1	cup finely chopped onions
$^1/_2$	cup finely chopped green peppers
$^1/_4$	cup finely chopped celery
1	teaspoon minced garlic
1	bay leaf
$1^1/_2$	teaspoons seafood seasoning
2	large eggs, divided
$^1/_3$	cup soft bread crumbs
1	cup crab claw meat
1	cup milk
$^1/_2$	cup all-purpose flour
$^1/_2$	cup clarified butter

Red Horseradish Sauce

1	small red bell pepper
1	cup sour cream
1	tablespoon prepared horseradish

PREPARATION

■ Melt butter in a heavy large sauté pan over medium heat. Add onions, green peppers, celery, garlic, bay leaf and seafood seasoning; sauté 10 to 15 minutes until vegetables are soft and tender. Set aside to cool; remove bay leaf.

■ In a bowl, beat 1 egg to combine. Add bread crumbs and cooled vegetable mixture; stir to thoroughly mix. Add crab meat and mix lightly so as to not break up the crab meat into small bits. Divide mixture into 8 parts; form into patties.

■ Beat remaining egg with a fork in a shallow flat dish such as a pie plate. Slowly add milk, whisking to combine. Place flour in a separate pie plate. Turn patties in flour to coat, dip in egg mixture, then coat with flour again. Heat $^1/_4$ cup clarified butter in a large sauté pan over medium heat. Panfry crab cakes until golden brown. Remove crab cakes to paper towels to drain. Repeat with remaining clarified butter and crab cakes. Serve with red horseradish sauce.

■ *To prepare the sauce:* Roast red pepper over a flame or under a broiler until skin is dark and blistered. Place in a plastic food storage bag and let stand 5 to 10 minutes. Peel pepper under running water. Remove seeds and stem; cut pepper into strips.

■ In a food processor, process pepper to a smooth purée. Add sour cream and horseradish; process until well blended.

• FOUR SERVINGS •

CRAWFISH ENCHILADA WITH SAUCE CON QUESO

. . . .

INGREDIENTS

2	teaspoons vegetable oil or bacon fat
2	teaspoons chili powder
¹/₂	cup finely chopped onion
¹/₄	cup finely chopped green bell pepper
¹/₄	cup finely chopped celery
2	teaspoons finely chopped garlic
2	teaspoons cornmeal
¹/₂	cup seafood stock or bottled clam juice
1¹/₂	cups heavy cream
¹/₂	cup shredded Cheddar cheese
	salt and pepper to taste
1	pound crawfish tails, peeled
8	corn tortillas
2	tablespoons chopped green onions
²/₃	cup shredded Monterey Jack cheese
	prepared salsa (optional)

PREPARATION

■ Heat oil in a medium saucepan over medium heat. Add chili powder, onion, bell pepper, celery and garlic; sauté about 10 minutes until vegetables are soft. Add cornmeal and cook another 2 minutes. Stir in stock and cream; bring mixture to a boil.

■ Remove pan from heat; add Cheddar cheese, stirring until melted. Season to taste with salt and pepper.

■ Heat oven to 400°F. Combine half the sauce with crawfish tails. Heat each tortilla about 20 seconds on high power in a microwave oven to soften.

■ Spoon crawfish mixture in the center of the tortilla, top with a few green onions and roll up. Place seam side down in a small baking dish. Repeat with remaining tortillas. Spoon on the remaining sauce and scatter the Monterey Jack cheese on top.

■ Bake about 20 minutes until the cheese starts to brown. Serve with salsa, if desired.

• FOUR SERVINGS •

Atlanta 1996

WERNER STANEK

Werner Stanek is executive chef at Château Élan Winery and
Resort in Braselton, Georgia. Chef Stanek studied pastry in Graz, Austria,
and did a hotel and resort apprenticeship at the Hotel Astoria
in Seefeld, Austria. Prior to joining Château Élan he worked in resorts
in Austria, Bermuda and the United States.

At Château Élan, Werner matches indigenous local ingredients
with his European training.

Chilled Yogurt Soup

Broiled Red Snapper with Mango &
Vidalia Onion Salsa

Cold Semolina Pudding

CHILLED YOGURT SOUP

INGREDIENTS

1	medium cucumber, pared
1	medium tomato, peeled, seeded and roughly chopped
3	tablespoons chopped Vidalia onions
2	tablespoons chopped mint
1	cup plain lowfat yogurt
1/2	teaspoon ground cumin
	salt and cayenne pepper
6	mint sprigs for garnish

PREPARATION

- In a food processor or blender, process the sliced cucumber, tomato, onions and mint until finely chopped. Add the yogurt and cumin; process to combine. Season with salt and cayenne pepper.

- Transfer soup to a bowl and refrigerate to chill. Serve cold garnished with mint.

• FOUR SERVINGS •

BROILED RED SNAPPER WITH MANGO & VIDALIA ONION SALSA

INGREDIENTS

1	medium mango, pared, diced
1/4	Vidalia onion, diced
1	teaspoon chopped mint
1	teaspoon lemon juice
	salt, pepper and sugar to taste
4	(6-ounce) skinless red snapper fillets
	olive oil

PREPARATION

- Combine mango, onion, mint and lemon juice in bowl; stir to mix. Season to taste with salt, pepper and sugar. Set aside for 1 hour for flavors to marry.

- Preheat broiler. Rinse fillets and pat dry with paper towels. Lightly oil fillets; season with salt and pepper. Broil 5 to 8 minutes until fish turns from translucent to opaque throughout. Serve with salsa.

• FOUR SERVINGS •

Atlanta 1996

COLD SEMOLINA PUDDING

· · · · · · · · · · · · · · · · · ·

INGREDIENTS

2	*cups milk*
1	*teaspoon vanilla extract*
¹/₂	*teaspoon salt*
¹/₂	*cup semolina flour*
1	*envelope unflavored gelatin*
2	*tablespoons cold water*
2	*egg yolks*
¹/₃	*cup sugar*
2	*cups heavy cream*
	sliced fresh fruit

PREPARATION

■ Bring milk, vanilla and salt to a boil in a heavy medium saucepan over high heat. Reduce the heat and with a wire whisk gradually whisk in the semolina flour. Cook, whisking almost constantly, 5 minutes. Meanwhile, combine the gelatin and water in a small bowl; set aside to soak. Whisk the egg yolks together in another small bowl.

■ Remove the pan from the heat; whisk about ¹/₂ cup of hot mixture into the yolks to warm them. Add the yolk mixture back to the pan, return the pan to the heat and cook 3 to 5 minutes longer until thickened. Whisk in sugar and softened gelatin; remove the pan from the heat to cool.

■ In a large mixing bowl with electric beaters, whip the cream until it forms soft peaks; fold the cooled mixture into the whipped cream. Spoon into six 1-cup molds. Refrigerate until set. To unmold, dip the molds in hot water and then invert. Serve pudding with fruit.

· SIX SERVINGS ·

RICK BAYLESS

Rick Bayless is chef-owner of Chicago's Fontera Grill,
one of this country's finest restaurants specializing in Mexican food.
Rick and wife Deann's fascination with Mexican cooking led them
throughout Mexico, where they added to their knowledge of
local ingredients and spices. Rick and Deann are authors of the highly
acclaimed cookbook *Authentic Mexican*, published by Morrow, and
Rick is host of the public television series "Cooking Mexican."

Beef & Potato Salad with Avocado & Chipotle Chiles

Mexican Sangria

Cinnamon-Vanilla Ice Cream

BEEF & POTATO SALAD WITH AVOCADO & CHIPOTLE CHILES

. . . .

INGREDIENTS

Dressing

1¹/₂	cups olive oil
¹/₂	cup cider vinegar
1	teaspoon salt
¹/₂	teaspoon ground black pepper

Salad

2	pounds flank steak, trimmed
1	large onion, diced
2	fresh serrano chiles, sliced
2	garlic cloves, peeled and quartered
2	bay leaves
1	teaspoon mixed dried herbs, such as oregano and thyme
	salt and pepper to taste
4	small round red-skin potatoes (³/₄ pounds), quartered
12	romaine lettuce leaves
2	avocados, sliced
8	canned chipotle chiles, halved and seeded
1	cup (4 ounces) crumbled Mexican queso fresco cheese
	radish roses, for garnish

PREPARATION

■ *To prepare the dressing:* Combine olive oil, vinegar, salt and black pepper in a jar with a tight-fitting lid. Shake, covered, until thoroughly blended.

■ *To prepare the salad and assemble:* Bring 1¹/₂ quarts of water to a boil in a large saucepan. Cut the flank steak into 2-inch squares. Add the meat to the water and skim off any grayish foam that rises to the top during the first minutes of boiling. Add half the onion, serrano chiles, garlic, bay leaves, dried herbs and salt and pepper to taste. Simmer over medium-low heat until tender, about 1 hour. Let meat cool in the broth. Drain; shred the meat into long thin strands.

■ While the meat cooks, boil the potatoes in salted water until tender, 10 to 15 minutes. Cool, peel off the skins and cut into ¹/₂-inch pieces. In a bowl, gently toss together the meat, potatoes, remaining onion and about ²/₃ of the dressing. Let stand, covered, 30 minutes. Season with salt and pepper.

■ Line a large platter with 8 romaine leaves; shred the remaining 4 to make a bed in the center. Scoop the meat mixture into the center of the platter. Arrange avocado slices and chipotle chiles around the edge. Drizzle with remaining dressing. Scatter cheese on top and garnish with radish roses.

NOTE: May substitute feta cheese for the fresco cheese.

• SIX SERVINGS •

MEXICAN SANGRIA

INGREDIENTS

$2/3$	cup sugar
$2/3$	cup fresh lime juice
$1/4$	cup water
3	cups dry fruity red wine
1	cup sparkling water
	ice
6	slices fresh lime, with a cut made on 1 side

PREPARATION

■ Stir together the sugar, lime juice and water until the sugar dissolves.

■ Just before serving, pour the wine into a pitcher; stir in the lime mixture, then sparkling water. Serve in tall glasses over ice. Garnish the rim of each glass with a circle of lime.

• SIX SERVINGS •

CINNAMON-VANILLA ICE CREAM

INGREDIENTS

4	cups milk
$1^{1}/2$	cups sugar
1	cinnamon stick
10	large egg yolks
1	teaspoon vanilla extract

PREPARATION

■ Stir together the milk, sugar and cinnamon stick in a large heavy saucepan. Bring the mixture to a boil, reduce the heat, cover and simmer 10 minutes. Remove the pan from the heat.

■ With a whisk, beat the egg yolks until runny. Slowly whisk about a cup of the hot milk mixture into the yolks; then whisk the yolk mixture back into the milk remaining in the saucepan. Cook over medium-low heat, stirring almost constantly, until the custard has thickened enough to coat a wooden spoon. Do not boil or the mixture will curdle.

■ Strain the custard through a fine mesh sieve, then stir in the vanilla. Cool to room temperature, then refrigerate to chill. Freeze in an ice cream maker following manufacturer's directions.

• SIX SERVINGS •

Atlanta 1996

GALE GAND & RICK TRAMONTO

Since the opening of their restaurants, Brasserie T and Trio, in Evanston, Illinois, Rick Tramonto and Gale Gand have fast become one of the nation's most celebrated chef couples. Within two years they were awarded a four-star rating by the *Chicago Tribune* (the first four-star rating given to a new restaurant in six years), the cover of *Chicago Magazine's* best new restaurants issue, *Food & Wine* magazine's Best New Chefs of 1994 award, the 1994 Robert Mondavi Award for Culinary Excellence, and a segment on the "America's Rising Star Chefs" PBS television series.

Gale and Rick both became interested in the restaurant business at early ages. Gale was studying silver and goldsmithing in college and took a year off from school to work in a restaurant. She soon discovered that the skills she learned in art translated well to cuisine, and she turned her talents to crafting beautiful breads and desserts. Rick, who started working for the Wendy's chain at age sixteen, went on to apprentice in some of the best kitchens in New York and then open a number of the most popular eateries in Chicago. At Trio, they feature contemporary fusion cuisine combining French and Italian cooking with an Asian influence.

Grilled Shrimp with Pesto Aioli

Osso Buco

Crème Brûlée Gale Gand

GRILLED SHRIMP WITH PESTO AIOLI

INGREDIENTS

1	*cup mayonnaise*
1	*teaspoon minced garlic*
1	*to 2 tablespoons lemon juice*
¹/₃	*cup pesto*
24	*large shrimp, peeled and deveined*
24	*thin slices pancetta*

PREPARATION

- In a mixing bowl, combine mayonnaise, garlic, lemon juice and pesto. Mix until well blended; adjust flavors to taste.

- Wrap each shrimp with a slice of pancetta; secure with a wooden pick. Grill shrimp over gas or charcoal until the pancetta is crisp and the shrimp are cooked through. Serve shrimp with pesto aioli.

NOTE: At the restaurant, Rick serves 4 shrimp on a plate, each accompanied by a different aioli: pesto aioli, roast garlic aioli, red pepper aioli and saffron aioli.

• SIX SERVINGS •

Atlanta 1996

OSSO BUCO

. . . .

INGREDIENTS

12	sections of veal shank, 2 inches thick
	salt and pepper to taste
1/4	cup olive oil
1/2	cup chopped carrots
1/2	cup chopped celery
1/2	cup chopped onion
1/4	cup tomato paste
1/2	cup red wine
1/2	cup orange juice
1/4	cup Pernod liqueur
2	tablespoons chopped fresh thyme
2	tablespoons chopped fresh rosemary
1	bay leaf
1/2	cup chopped shallots
1/2	head garlic, cloves peeled
4	cups veal or beef stock

Garnish

1/2	cup finely chopped Italian flat-leaf parsley
	grated zest of 1 lemon
	grated zest of 1 orange

PREPARATION

■ Heat oven to 350°F. Season veal shanks with salt and pepper. Heat oil in a large flameproof casserole or Dutch oven over medium-high heat and quickly sear the veal, browning it well on all sides. Transfer to paper towels to drain.

■ Add carrots, celery and onion to the casserole and cook, stirring occasionally, until vegetables brown and start to caramelize. Stir in tomato paste, then red wine, orange juice and liqueur. Bring the mixture to a boil, scraping the bottom of the pan. Boil to reduce by half. Return the veal shanks to the casserole with the remaining ingredients and bring to a boil. Season to taste with salt and pepper.

■ Cover the casserole, transfer to the oven, and bake for 2 hours or longer until the veal is very tender. Garnish each serving with chopped parsley and lemon and orange zests.

NOTE: Rick serves the Osso Buco with orzo pasta cooked with a pinch of saffron.

• SIX SERVINGS •

CREME BRULEE GALE GAND

. . . .

INGREDIENTS

3¹/₂	*cups heavy cream*
¹/₂	*cup half-and-half*
1	*vanilla bean, split*
12	*egg yolks*
³/₄	*cup sugar*
¹/₄	*cup shaved semisweet chocolate*
	brown sugar
	chocolate straws (optional)
	powdered sugar

Grape & Raspberry Mint Salad

2	*cups small seedless grapes*
2	*cups raspberries*
¹/₂	*cup raspberry purée*
4	*mint leaves, finely shredded*

PREPARATION

■ Heat oven to 300°F. Combine cream, half-and-half and vanilla bean in a medium saucepan; bring to a boil. Remove pan from the heat. Whisk yolks together in a mixing bowl with sugar. Pour about a cup of hot cream into yolks to warm, then pour the entire mixture back into a saucepan.

■ Cook, stirring, over medium heat until mixture thickens to a custard-like consistency. Strain through a wire mesh sieve. Ladle custard into eight 6-ounce soufflé dishes or ramekins. Scatter shaved chocolate on top. Place dishes in a baking pan; fill pan with enough water to come halfway up the sides of the soufflé dishes. Bake about 30 minutes until a knife inserted near the center of the dish comes out clean. Cool on wire racks, then refrigerate to chill.

■ At serving, preheat the broiler. Sprinkle a thin layer of brown sugar over the custards and place them under the broiler just until the sugar caramelizes, 2 to 4 minutes. Serve immediately with grape & raspberry mint salad and an additional garnish of chocolate straws and powdered sugar, if desired.

■ *To prepare the salad:* Gently toss together all ingredients in a bowl. Makes 4 cups.

• EIGHT SERVINGS •

JACK PANDL

Jack Pandl has followed the restaurant tradition his parents began
in 1915 when they bought the Whitefish Bay Inn in
Milwaukee, Wisconsin. The inn is surrounded by homes today, but
eighty years ago the area was occupied only by farms and the
old Pabst Whitefish Bay Resort—a fairground of beer gardens,
picnic tables and a dance pavilion.

One of the few Milwaukee-area restaurants to endure the test of
time at its original location, Jack Pandl's Whitefish Bay Inn is
virtually a landmark, reminiscent of an unhurried past. The building's
appearance has remained basically unchanged since 1915.
Inside, Tiffany lamps, oak tables, fresh flowers and antique beer steins
enhance the cozy charm of the dining rooms.

The menu at Pandl's has changed since its early days,
but the culinary influence of Jack's mother, Anna Pandl, remains.
Today Jack's children are involved in the restaurant, preserving
the family tradition.

Cool Cucumber Soup

Broiled Whitefish

Jack Pandl's Famous German Pancake

COOL CUCUMBER SOUP

. . . .

INGREDIENTS

1¹/₂	tablespoons butter
¹/₂	medium onion, finely chopped
1	leek, thinly sliced
2	cups chicken stock
4	cups diced cucumber
¹/₂	cup peeled diced potato
¹/₄	teaspoon dry mustard
1	cup half-and-half
	salt and white pepper

Garnishes

finely diced radishes

finely diced cucumber

chopped chives

watercress leaves

PREPARATION

■ Melt butter in a large heavy saucepan over medium heat. Add onion and leek; sauté until onion is translucent. Add chicken stock, cucumber, potato and mustard; simmer until potato is tender.

■ Purée mixture in batches in a blender. Cool puréed soup, then refrigerate to chill. Stir in half-and-half. Season to taste with salt and white pepper. Serve soup chilled with garnishes sprinkled on top.

• SIX SERVINGS •

BROILED WHITEFISH

. . . .

INGREDIENTS

6	*(8-ounce) whitefish fillets*
	vegetable oil
	salt and pepper
	paprika
	lemon wedges
	parsley sprigs

PREPARATION

■ Debone the fillets by first laying them skin-side down on a work surface. Gently run your fingers across the fillets from head to tail to raise the bones, then use needle-nose pliers to pull out the bones. Rinse the fillets and pat dry with paper towels.

■ Preheat the broiler. Oil a baking sheet and brush the fillets with oil. Season with salt and pepper. Broil 8 to 10 minutes until opaque throughout. Sprinkle with paprika. Serve with lemon wedges and parsley.

• SIX SERVINGS •

JACK PANDL'S FAMOUS GERMAN PANCAKE

. . . .

INGREDIENTS

½	*cup all-purpose flour*
½	*cup milk*
	pinch salt
4	*large eggs*
1	*tablespoon butter*
1	*tablespoon vegetable shortening*
	butter
	lemon wedges
	maple syrup
	powdered sugar

PREPARATION

■ Heat oven to 425°F. Whisk together the flour, milk and salt in a mixing bowl. Add the eggs and whisk until blended and smooth. Melt 1 tablespoon butter and shortening in a 9- or 10-inch ovenproof skillet; tilt the pan to coat skillet. Add batter and cook over medium heat until the bottom of the pancake has browned, 4 to 5 minutes. With a spatula, lift edge of the pancake and tilt the pan to let the uncooked batter on top fall into the skillet. Turn pancake and make several cuts all the way through with a knife.

■ Place the skillet in the oven for 12 minutes or until the edges brown and the pancake has risen. Serve immediately with butter, a squeeze of lemon, maple syrup and powdered sugar.

NOTE: Pancake can be served as a meal for one or a dessert for several.

• ONE PANCAKE •

CHARLES WEBER

Charles Weber has worked his way up through restaurant and hotel kitchens from coast to coast. In 1994 he opened the Park Avenue Cafe in Chicago, Illinois, which has received rave reviews from critics and customers alike. The chef's forte is with wine and food combinations— matching the right wine to his particular dishes.

Charles is a founding member of the Chicago Chef's Alliance, a national chairperson for Chefs in America, and a member of the National Board of Directors for the National Executive Chefs' Association.

Sweet-Herb-Seared Halibut with Three-Bean Salad

*Fillet of Yellow Tail Snapper Steamed in
Napa Cabbage & Scallion Vinaigrette*

Atlanta 1996

SWEET-HERB-SEARED HALIBUT WITH THREE-BEAN SALAD

INGREDIENTS

6	(6- to 8-ounce) skinless fillets of halibut
	olive oil
	salt and pepper to taste
1/2	cup combination of finely chopped fresh herbs, such as parsley, chives, tarragon, sage, basil, dill and mint*
2	tablespoons olive oil

Three-Bean Salad

1	cup sherry vinegar
2	chipotle chile peppers
1	cup olive oil
1	cup cooked black beans
1	cup cooked navy beans
1	cup blanched green beans
1/2	cup diced bell pepper, preferably a combination of red and green peppers
1/4	cup coarsely chopped cilantro
	salt and pepper to taste

* In the restaurant, Charles uses a combination of tarragon, pineapple sage, cinnamon basil, dill and apple mint.

PREPARATION

- Rinse fillets and pat dry with paper towels. Brush with olive oil and season with salt and pepper. Place finely chopped herbs on a plate and turn fillets in herbs to lightly coat.

- Heat 1 tablespoon olive oil in each of 2 sauté pans or skillets. Add halibut and cook over medium heat, 3 to 5 minutes per side, until fish turns from translucent to opaque throughout. Serve with three-bean salad.

- *To prepare the three-bean salad:* Bring the vinegar and chile peppers to a boil in a medium saucepan. Remove from heat and set aside to cool. Strain vinegar into a bowl; whisk in olive oil.

- In a separate bowl, toss together beans, bell peppers and cilantro. Add enough vinegar-oil mixture to coat, about 1 cup. Toss and season to taste with salt and pepper.

• SIX SERVINGS •

FILLET OF YELLOW TAIL SNAPPER STEAMED IN NAPA CABBAGE & SCALLION VINAIGRETTE

INGREDIENTS

8	*(6- to 8-ounce) skinless fillets of red snapper*
	salt and pepper
1	*large head Napa cabbage*

Scallion Vinaigrette

6	*green onions, thinly sliced*
1	*cup rice wine vinegar*
1½	*teaspoons soy sauce*
1	*small hot red pepper, finely chopped*
1	*teaspoon minced garlic*
1	*teaspoon grated or minced fresh ginger*
1	*tablespoon toasted sesame oil*
1	*cup grapeseeds or peanut oil*
	salt and pepper to taste

PREPARATION

■ Rinse fillets and pat dry with paper towels; season with salt and pepper. Bring a large saucepan of water to a boil. Pull the large outer leaves off the cabbage and immerse in boiling water. Boil 1 minute, then plunge into a bowl of ice water to stop the cooking. Wrap the fillets in cabbage leaves. Place fillets on a steamer rack. Cover; steam over simmering water 5 to 8 minutes until fish turns from translucent to opaque throughout. Serve with scallion vinaigrette.

■ *To prepare the vinaigrette:* Combine green onions, vinegar, soy sauce, red pepper, garlic and ginger in a bowl. With a wire whisk, whisk in oils. Season to taste with salt and pepper.

• EIGHT SERVINGS •

CHRIS WILLIAMS

Chris Williams is the owner of the Courtesy Coffee Shop
in Winchester, Indiana. He writes:

"My purchase of the Courtesy Coffee Shop is without question the
highlight of my career. The Courtesy opened in Winchester, Indiana,
(population 5,000) in 1947. It was purchased by my Great Aunt Ann
Vance in 1949 and made into a cafeteria because 'everyone seems to be in
such a hurry.' Aunt Ann moved the Courtesy in 1954 to the Randolph
Hotel, filling its vacant kitchen and dining room. The hotel was built
in 1904. I purchased the Courtesy in 1990 when Aunt Ann finally decided
to retire. She worked every day and was in her 80s.

"The Courtesy is a very special place. Time has stopped here.
It's obvious in the atmosphere and more importantly the food. We don't
really desire to be trendy. Everything is as it is because nothing
ever changes at the Courtesy.

"By printing I expect for the Courtesy to have completed its last move.
We are trading in our 3,400 square feet for 10,000 square feet in a former
department store building. The building operated as the W. E. Miller
department store from 1883 to 1938, and the Boston Store from 1938 to
1980. It's a grand old building by Winchester standards, and the perfect
place for a grand old eatery by anyone's standards."

Sirloin Beef Tips in Red Wine

Courtesy Creamed Peas

Old-Fashioned Sugar Cream Pie

SIRLOIN BEEF TIPS IN RED WINE

INGREDIENTS

1	slice bacon, cut into small pieces
2	pounds sirloin beef tips or stew beef
2	cups dry red wine, preferably Burgundy, divided
1	cup beef broth
1	tablespoon tomato paste
1	teaspoon salt
1	teaspoon minced garlic
1/2	teaspoon dried marjoram leaves
1	tablespoon finely chopped parsley
1	bay leaf, broken in half
3	tablespoons flour
1/2	pound tiny white onions, peeled
1	pound baby carrots
2	pounds tiny red potatoes
1/2	pound small mushrooms, cut in half

PREPARATION

■ Heat oven to 375°F. Cook bacon until crisp in a large flameproof casserole over medium-high heat. Remove bacon, leaving fat in casserole. Add beef and brown on all sides. Remove beef and set aside. Add 1 1/2 cups red wine, the beef broth, tomato paste, salt, garlic, marjoram, parsley and bay leaf to the casserole. Bring to a boil.

■ Whisk together the flour and remaining 1/2 cup wine; add to the liquid in casserole. Add the beef, bacon and vegetables to the casserole. Cover and bake 1 1/2 to 2 hours until beef is tender.

NOTE: "This is one of my own favorite recipes that is now served at the Courtesy. It gives me such joy to serve because it smells up the kitchen divinely, and our customers love it. I think of it as a rich man's pot roast, but it doesn't have to be expensive. A nice variation is to skip the potatoes and carrots, bake the meat by itself, and serve on wide egg noodles or rice pilaf with broccoli."

• FIVE TO SIX SERVINGS •

Atlanta 1996

COURTESY CREAMED PEAS

INGREDIENTS

1	pound green peas, fresh or frozen
1	cup water
2	cups half-and-half
1	teaspoon salt
1/4	cup (1/2 stick) butter
1/4	cup sugar
1/4	cup cornstarch dissolved in 1/2 cup cold water

PREPARATION

■ In a large heavy saucepan, combine peas, water, half-and-half, salt, butter and sugar over medium heat and bring almost to a boil.

■ Slowly add cornstarch mixture and cook, stirring, until the mixture thickens to the consistency of gravy.

NOTE: "This recipe has always been a closely guarded secret, as were all the recipes by my Great Aunt Ann. She always brought creamed peas to family gatherings. At one family gathering her daughter thought she would save her mom the trouble of bringing them, so she asked how to make them. The reply was 'You don't need to know!' When I bought the Courtesy the cooks whispered recipes in my ear so the pot and pan washer working nearby couldn't hear."

• SIX SERVINGS •

OLD-FASHIONED SUGAR CREAM PIE

INGREDIENTS

1 1/3	cups sifted all-purpose flour
1	cup sugar
2/3	cup half-and-half
2 2/3	cups heavy cream
	unbaked 10-inch pie shell
	ground nutmeg

PREPARATION

■ Heat oven to 400°F. Stir together flour and sugar in a mixing bowl. Stir in half-and-half until blended, then stir in cream. Pour the filling into the pie shell. Sprinkle the nutmeg over the filling along the edge. With a spoon, stir the filling in a clockwise motion, starting along the edge to swirl the nutmeg into the filling.

■ Cover the edge of the pie shell loosely with foil. Bake 15 minutes. Reduce oven temperature to 300°F. Remove the foil and bake about 30 minutes longer until the center has thickened. Cool on a wire rack 2 hours before serving.

• EIGHT SERVINGS •

SOUTHWEST

BRUCE AUDEN

Bruce Auden is chef/owner of Restaurant BIGA and LocuStreet Bakery in
San Antonio, Texas, along with his wife, artisan baker Debra Auden.
When the restaurant opened in 1991, *Esquire* magazine listed BIGA as one
of the best new restaurants that year. In 1994, Bruce and Debra were
recognized as Entrepreneurs of the Year for the south Texas region.

The restaurant features a daily changing menu that the chef describes as
"eclectic, contemporary American Cuisine." BIGA's wine list boasts
over 300 international wines and micro-brewed beers to accompany
Bruce and Debra's cuisine and rustic breads.

Walnut, Beet, Grapefruit & Endive Salad

Gulf Flounder à la Plancha

Key Lime Delicious

Atlanta 1996

WALNUT, BEET, GRAPEFRUIT & ENDIVE SALAD

. . . .

INGREDIENTS

Garlic Oil

2	cups corn oil
24	garlic cloves, peeled

Grapefruit & Sherry Vinaigrette

	juice of 1 grapefruit
	juice of 1 lemon
	juice of 1 orange
1	tablespoon sugar
1	tablespoon finely grated grapefruit zest
1	tablespoon apple cider vinegar
1	tablespoon sherry vinegar
3/4	cup olive oil
	salt and pepper to taste

Salad

2	heads Belgium endive
3	bunches watercress
1 1/2	pounds beets, cooked, peeled and cut into thin wedges
3	ruby grapefruit, cut into sections
2/3	cup walnut halves, lightly toasted
2	tablespoons walnut oil

PREPARATION

- *To prepare the garlic oil:* Heat corn oil and garlic cloves in a medium saucepan over medium heat for about 30 minutes. Cool to room temperature. Strain and reserve both oil and garlic.

- *To prepare the vinaigrette:* Combine citrus juices and sugar in a small pan over medium-high heat. Bring to a boil and cook to reduce to 2 tablespoons; cool. Add grapefruit zest and vinegars. Whisk in olive oil and 1/4 cup of the reserved garlic oil. Season to taste with salt and pepper.

- *To prepare the salad and serve:* Arrange endive leaves on a plate in a square like Lincoln logs. Fill center loosely with watercress. Arrange beets and grapefruit sections on watercress and drizzle with 3/4 cup of the vinaigrette. Sprinkle walnut halves over salad and drizzle with walnut oil.

• SIX SERVINGS •

GULF FLOUNDER A LA PLANCHA

. . . .

INGREDIENTS

Plancha Seasoning

¹/₄	cup ground pasilla pepper
1	tablespoon ground black pepper
1	tablespoon ground paprika
1¹/₂	teaspoons ground white pepper
1¹/₂	teaspoons dried crushed oregano leaves
1¹/₂	teaspoons salt

Flounder

2	tablespoons olive oil
1	pound porcini mushrooms, sliced
	salt
6	(6- to 8-ounce) skinless flounder fillets
	olive oil
8	garlic cloves, thinly sliced
6	chile arbol or pinch cayenne pepper
¹/₂	cup (1 stick) butter
¹/₂	cup lemon juice
12	chervil or parsley sprigs

PREPARATION

■ *To prepare the seasoning:* Blend together all seasoning ingredients. Makes about ¹/₂ cup.

■ *To prepare the flounder and serve:* Heat 2 tablespoons olive oil over medium-high heat in a cast-iron skillet. Add mushrooms and sauté until browned. Remove and reserve. Sprinkle a little salt in the skillet. Rinse fillets; pat dry with paper towels. Brush with olive oil and sprinkle with plancha seasoning.

■ Cook 3 or 4 fillets at a time, turning when brown. Remove to a platter and keep warm in the oven. Add the sautéed mushrooms, garlic, chile arbol and butter to the skillet; cook over high heat until the butter just starts to brown. Add the lemon juice and chervil. Remove chiles. Spoon mushroom sauce over fillets.

NOTE: At the restaurant, Bruce serves the fish on a bed of mashed potatoes and baked artichokes.

• SIX SERVINGS •

KEY LIME DELICIOUS

· ·

INGREDIENTS

2	*tablespoons butter, softened*
2	*cups sugar*
¹/₄	*cup all-purpose flour*
	juice of 5 key limes
1	*tablespoon finely grated lime zest*
2	*cups milk*
4	*egg yolks, slightly beaten*
4	*egg whites*
	crème fraîche

PREPARATION

■ Heat oven to 250°F. In a mixing bowl with electric beaters, beat together butter and sugar until blended. Add flour, lime juice, lime zest, milk and egg yolks; beat until smooth and blended.

■ In a separate bowl, beat egg whites until they hold soft peaks. Fold whites into batter.

■ Pour the mixture into a 1½-quart baking dish. Place the baking dish in a 9x13-inch pan and fill with hot water to come halfway up the sides of the baking dish. Bake 1 hour until the top is firm. Serve warm or at room temperature with chilled crème fraîche.

· SIX SERVINGS ·

MICHAEL CORDUA

Michael Cordua is chef/owner of two of the most popular restaurants in Houston, Texas: Churrascos South American Restaurant and Americas. Michael has been recognized as developing a unique South American-style cuisine starting with the native ingredients of his homeland, Nicaragua, and utilizing a combination of classic French and American cooking preparations.

Born in Managua, Nicaragua, Michael was educated at Texas A&M University, and graduated in 1980 with a degree in economics and finance. A self-taught chef, he always had an affinity for cooking for his large circle of friends and family. One of eight children, Michael became the family's "chef" for special occasions, learning recipes and techniques from his mother and the family's cook.

In 1988 Michael opened Churrascos, Texas' first restaurant specializing in fine South American cuisine. In 1993 he opened Americas, specializing in the foods of all the Americas, North, Central and South. In 1993 Americas was named Restaurant of the Year by *Esquire* magazine.

In 1994 Michael was named one of America's Ten Best New Chefs by *Food & Wine* magazine. He was also selected as one of thirteen recipients of the 1994 Robert Mondavi Awards for Culinary Excellence.

Hongos Rellenos

Pechugas Bahía

Flan de Queso

HONGOS RELLENOS

. . . .

INGREDIENTS

18	large mushroom caps
18	large sea scallops
	salt and pepper
	olive oil
	finely diced red bell pepper and chopped cilantro leaves for garnish

Huancaina Sauce

1	tablespoon olive oil
1/4	white onion, chopped
1/2	aji pepper*, chopped
1/4	cup evaporated milk
1 1/2	cups whipping cream
1/4	cup dry sherry
1/2	cup cotija cheese*
2	teaspoons cornstarch dissolved in 2 tablespoons cold water

* Aji peppers and cotija cheese can be found in Hispanic grocery stores.

PREPARATION

■ Season mushrooms and scallops with salt and pepper. Brush with olive oil. Grill the scallops for 4 minutes. Grill the mushrooms for 2 minutes.

■ Spoon a pool of huancaina sauce on each of 6 small serving plates. Place scallops inside mushroom caps and arrange 3 on each plate. Shower edge of plates with red pepper and cilantro.

■ *To prepare the huancaina sauce:* Heat olive oil in a sauté pan over medium-high heat; add onion and aji pepper and sauté until onion is translucent. Place onion, pepper, evaporated milk and cream in a blender; process until smooth. Strain mixture through a wire mesh sieve and transfer to a saucepan. Add sherry and cheese. Stir in cornstarch mixture; heat over medium heat, stirring constantly until sauce thickens. Strain again.

NOTE: For extra flavor, place 6 to 8 corn husk leaves in the bottom of the grill to create smoke.

• SIX SERVINGS •

PECHUGAS BAHIA

INGREDIENTS

6	*boneless skinless chicken breasts*
	salt and pepper
1/4	*cup virgin olive oil*
1	*tablespoon finely chopped garlic*
3/4	*cup unsweetened coconut milk*
1/2	*cup (1 stick) butter, softened*
	juice of 1 lime
3/4	*cup chopped seeded tomatoes*
1	*jalapeño pepper, seeded, veined, finely chopped*
6	*large (1x5-inch) hearts of palm, sliced thinly on the diagonal*
3/4	*cup chopped cilantro*

PREPARATION

■ Season chicken with salt and pepper. Mix together oil and garlic. Grill chicken, basting with garlic-oil mixture, until chicken is cooked through; keep warm.

■ In a medium saucepan over low heat, warm (don't boil) coconut milk and slowly add butter, whisking to incorporate. Remove from heat; add lime juice, chopped tomatoes, jalapeño and hearts of palm. Season with salt and adjust flavors to taste. Place each breast on a plate; spoon on sauce. Sprinkle with chopped cilantro.

• SIX SERVINGS •

FLAN DE QUESO

INGREDIENTS

3	*large eggs*
2	*egg yolks*
1	*can (14 ounces) sweetened condensed milk*
1³/₄	*cups milk*
1¹/₂	*teaspoons vanilla extract*
5	*ounces cream cheese, softened*
1	*cup sugar*
2	*tablespoons water*

PREPARATION

■ Heat oven to 250° F. In a blender, whirl eggs, egg yolks, sweetened condensed milk, milk, vanilla extract and cream cheese until smooth. Blend 2 more minutes.

■ In a heavy saucepan, melt sugar over medium heat; continue heating until sugar caramelizes and turns golden brown. Add water; stir to combine.

■ Pour caramelized sugar into the bottoms of six 6-ounce ovenproof ramekins. Pour custard into dishes. Set ramekins in a large pan; add hot water to come about halfway up the sides. Bake, uncovered, for 50 to 60 minutes until flans are firm.

• SIX SERVINGS •

ROBERT DEL GRANDE

Robert Del Grande is one of the celebrated chefs of America
and is chef/partner at Cafe Annie in Houston, Texas. Robert received his
undergraduate degree in chemistry and biology, and a Ph.D.
in biochemistry. Experiments in the kitchen soon took precedence
over experiments in the lab, and Robert became executive chef
at Cafe Annie, where he developed his American cooking
with a Southwestern edge.

Robert has received numerous culinary awards and honors. In 1992
alone he received the James Beard Award, the Ivy Award
(*Restaurant & Institutions* magazine), the Distinguished Restaurants
Award (*Condé Nast Traveler*), and the Distinguished Restaurants
of North America (DiRoNA) Award. In addition, he has been
named to the Fine Dining Hall of Fame (*Nation's Restaurant News*),
Who's Who of Cooking in Texas, and Honor Roll of American
Chefs (*Food & Wine* magazine).

Mango, Sweet Pepper & Grilled Red Onion Salad

*Pork Loin Chops in Tomato Mushroom Sauce
with Polenta*

Blackberry & Pound Cake Crisp

Atlanta 1996

MANGO, SWEET PEPPER & GRILLED RED ONION SALAD

INGREDIENTS

2	*red bell peppers*
2	*red onions, sliced crosswise about ¼ inch thick*
2	*ripe mangoes*
1	*small bunch cilantro*
3	*tablespoons olive oil*
1	*tablespoon lime juice*
	salt and freshly cracked black pepper
4	*small bunches arugula*

PREPARATION

■ Roast peppers over a charcoal grill or gas fire until skins are dark and blistered. Place in a paper or plastic food storage bag; close top. Set aside 5 to 10 minutes. Peel blistered peppers. Under running water, skins remove easily. Cut in quarters; remove seeds and stem; set aside.

■ Grill the onions until lightly browned; set aside. Pare the mangoes and cut the fruit in thick slices from the seed. Combine the peppers, onions and mango slices in a bowl. Add sprigs of cilantro. Add oil, lime juice and salt and pepper to taste. Arrange arugula on 4 salad plates; top with mango mixture.

• FOUR SERVINGS •

PORK LOIN CHOPS IN TOMATO MUSHROOM SAUCE WITH POLENTA

INGREDIENTS

2	**tablespoons olive oil, divided**
4	**pork loin chops**
	salt and pepper to taste
$\frac{1}{2}$	**white onion, chopped**
4	**garlic cloves, chopped**
1	**tablespoon fennel seeds**
$\frac{1}{2}$	**pound fresh mushrooms, sliced**
2	**cans (14 ounces) whole peeled tomatoes in juice, undrained**
1	**cup water**
1	**tablespoon finely chopped sage**
	salt to taste
1	**teaspoon freshly ground black peppercorns**
1	**tablespoon finely chopped parsley**
	finely grated Parmesan cheese

Polenta

2	**cups water**
1	**teaspoon salt**
$\frac{1}{2}$	**cup polenta or very coarsely ground cornmeal**

PREPARATION

■ Heat 1 tablespoon oil in a large heavy pot over medium-high heat. Lightly season pork chops with salt and pepper to taste. Sear chops on both sides until browned, about 2 to 3 minutes per side. Remove from the pot and reserve.

■ Heat the remaining tablespoon of oil in the pot. Add the onion, garlic and fennel seeds; sauté until onion is translucent. Add mushrooms and sauté 2 to 3 minutes until just cooked through. Add tomatoes with juice, water, sage, salt to taste or up to 1 teaspoon salt and 1 teaspoon fresh ground black peppercorns. Bring the liquid to a boil, lower the heat and simmer 30 minutes. As the tomatoes simmer, break some up into pieces with a spoon. The sauce should be chunky.

■ Add the pork chops to the simmering sauce. Cover the pot and simmer 10 to 15 minutes until the pork is cooked but still slightly pink in the center. Stir in the parsley. Serve the pork chops and sauce over the polenta. Top with Parmesan cheese.

■ *To prepare the polenta:* Bring the water and salt to a boil in a large saucepan over medium-high heat. Add the polenta in a steady stream while whisking vigorously. Bring the polenta to a boil, lower the heat and simmer gently for about 30 minutes, stirring frequently. Cover and keep warm.

• FOUR SERVINGS •

Atlanta 1996

BLACKBERRY & POUND CAKE CRISP

. . . .

INGREDIENTS

Pound Cake

1	cup sugar
1	cup (2 sticks) unsalted butter, softened
4	ounces cream cheese, softened
1	tablespoon vanilla extract
6	egg yolks
1½	cups all-purpose flour
1	teaspoon baking power
1	teaspoon salt
6	egg whites

Crisp Topping

1	cup all-purpose flour
¾	cup packed light brown sugar
½	teaspoon salt
½	teaspoon cinnamon
½	cup cold unsalted butter, cut into small cubes

Blackberries

4	cups blackberries
2	tablespoons all-purpose flour
2	tablespoons sugar
⅓	cup heavy whipping cream

PREPARATION

- *To prepare the pound cake:* Heat oven to 300°F. Beat sugar and butter with an electric mixer until light and fluffy. Add the cream cheese and vanilla and mix to thoroughly incorporate. With the mixer running, add the egg yolks 1 at a time and beat until fully incorporated. Combine the flour, baking powder and salt; add to butter mixture and mix to blend.

- In a separate bowl, beat egg whites until they hold soft peaks. Stir ⅓ of the whites into the batter to lighten it, then fold in the remaining whites. Scrape the batter into a buttered loaf pan.

- Bake 1 hour or until a wooden pick inserted in the center comes out clean. Allow to cool on a wire rack.

- *To prepare the crisp topping:* In a bowl, stir together the flour, brown sugar, salt and cinnamon to blend. Add the butter and mix with electric beaters or your fingers until the ingredients come together in a moist, coarse dough.

- *To assemble and bake:* Heat the oven to 350°F. Cut four or five ½-inch slices from the pound cake. Lightly toast the slices in a toaster oven or under a broiler. Break the toasted slices into quarters and arrange in a single layer in the bottom of a 9-inch square glass baking dish.

- Toss together the blackberries, flour and sugar in a bowl; pour the berry mixture over the pound cake layer. Drizzle the cream over the berries. Crumble the crisp topping over the top. Bake 45 to 50 minutes until the topping is crisp. Allow to cool 15 minutes on a wire rack, then serve warm.

• SIX TO EIGHT SERVINGS •

DEAN FEARING

Dean Fearing, chef of the Mansion on Turtle Creek in
Dallas, Texas, can be found buzzing around the kitchen in chef's whites
and Lucchese cowboy boots. A chef who has been at the forefront
in developing Southwestern cuisine, Dean blends seasonal
native ingredients with flavors and cooking techniques from around
the world: Texas-grown chili peppers, jicama, cilantro, native
herbs and tomatillos, along with Texas Hill Country wild game, birds and
venison, infused with concepts and techniques from Italian,
Thai and Mexican cuisines.

Dean is the author of two cookbooks: *The Mansion on Turtle Creek
Cookbook* and *Dean Fearing's Southwest Cuisine: Blending Asia and
the Americas*. He is the recipient of numerous culinary awards, including
the recent Robb Report 1994 Best U.S. Restaurant Award and the 1994
James Beard Restaurant Award for Best Chef, Southwest.

*Skillet-Fried Corn Bread
with Spicy Shrimp & Crab Meat*

Orange & Jicama Salad

Butterfinger Candy Bar Pie

Atlanta 1996

SKILLET-FRIED CORN BREAD WITH SPICY SHRIMP & CRAB MEAT

INGREDIENTS

Skillet-Fried Corn Bread

2	cups yellow cornmeal
1	teaspoon each sugar and salt
1	tablespoon bacon fat or oil
1/4	cup buttermilk
1 1/2	to 2 cups boiling water
	corn oil for frying

Spicy Shrimp & Crab Meat

1 1/2	cups heavy cream
1 1/2	cups chicken stock
1	tablespoon olive oil
16	large shrimp, peeled, deveined
	salt to taste
1/2	each red, green and yellow bell peppers, seeded, cut into 1/2-inch squares
2	serrano chiles, seeded, chopped
2	garlic cloves, minced
2	shallots, finely chopped
2	teaspoons paprika
1/4	cup sherry
6	ounces crab meat
	lemon juice
	cilantro sprigs for garnish

PREPARATION

■ *To prepare the corn bread:* Combine cornmeal, sugar and salt in a mixing bowl. Add bacon fat, buttermilk and boiling water; stir to blend. Pour oil to a depth of 1/2 inch in a cast-iron skillet and heat over medium-high heat to 325°F.

■ Drop large spoonfuls of cornmeal batter into hot oil. Fry for 5 to 7 minutes, turning to brown on all sides. Remove pieces from skillet and drain on paper towels.

■ *To prepare the spicy shrimp and crab meat:* Bring cream and chicken stock to a boil in a medium saucepan over high heat; boil 5 to 7 minutes until reduced to about 1 1/2 cups. Set aside.

■ Heat oil in a large sauté pan over medium-high heat. Season shrimp with salt and add to pan; sauté 2 minutes. Add peppers and sauté 2 more minutes. Add chiles, garlic, shallots and paprika; sauté 1 minute. Add sherry and cook 1 to 2 minutes until almost evaporated. Stir in cream mixture; cook to heat through. Stir in crab meat, then season to taste with lemon juice and salt.

■ *To assemble:* Place corn bread at "two," "six," and "ten" o'clock positions on each of 4 serving plates. Spoon seafood mixture into the center of each plate. Garnish with cilantro.

• FOUR SERVINGS •

ORANGE & JICAMA SALAD

INGREDIENTS

¹⁄₄	cup olive oil
¹⁄₄	cup peanut oil
¹⁄₄	cup fresh lime juice
¹⁄₂	teaspoon each cayenne pepper, ground cumin and ground coriander
4	medium seedless oranges
1	large red onion
1¹⁄₂	cups julienne-cut jicama
¹⁄₄	cup chopped cilantro plus sprigs for garnish

PREPARATION

■ In a bowl, whisk together olive oil, peanut oil, lime juice, cayenne pepper, ground cumin, ground coriander and salt to taste.

■ Peel oranges and cut each crosswise into 4 slices. Cut onion crosswise into 12 thin slices. Place an orange slice in the middle of each of 4 salad plates. Top with red onion slices, a few pieces of jicama and a little chopped cilantro. Spoon on about 1¹⁄₂ teaspoons dressing. Repeat layering of orange, onion, jicama and cilantro until all ingredients are used. Spoon additional dressing over the top. Garnish with cilantro sprigs.

• FOUR SERVINGS •

BUTTERFINGER CANDY BAR PIE

INGREDIENTS

8	Butterfinger candy bars
2	large eggs
1¹⁄₂	cups sugar
¹⁄₂	cup water
¹⁄₄	cup all-purpose flour
¹⁄₄	teaspoon salt
¹⁄₂	cup unsalted butter, melted
	unbaked 9-inch pie shell
	whipped cream

PREPARATION

■ Chop 6 candy bars; set aside. Chop remaining 2 candy bars; set aside. Whisk eggs in a large mixing bowl. Add sugar, water, flour and salt; mix to blend. Stir in melted butter, then stir in 6 chopped candy bars. Refrigerate mixture for 8 hours.

■ Heat oven to 325°F. Scrape filling into unbaked pie shell. Bake 45 minutes. Cool on a wire rack, then refrigerate 12 hours or overnight. Serve garnished with whipped cream and remaining chopped candy bars.

• EIGHT SERVINGS •

FLORENCE JARAMILLO

Florence and Arturo Jaramillo, the founders of Rancho de Chimayó,
twenty-five miles north of Santa Fe, New Mexico, envisioned it
as a living tribute to the Spanish American heritage of New Mexico.
In addition to the native cooking of the area, Rancho de Chimayó
serves its guests a way of life.

In 1965 the Jaramillos converted Arturo's grandparents' home
into the restaurant. Using old family recipes, they fashioned the food after
meals Arturo had as a child. Rancho de Chimayó was one of the first
restaurants to offer "New Mexican" food based on local preparations and
ingredients and is known for specialties of the area, such as posole,
carne adovado and sopaipillas.

Today, daughter Laura Ann Jaramillo and cousin Dan Jaramillo run the
restaurant with Florence and continue the traditions of the ranch.

Red Chile Sauce

Tortilla Soup

RED CHILE SAUCE

INGREDIENTS

8	*ounces lean ground beef*
3/4	*cup dried ground red chile, such as Chimayó or ancho*
1	*tablespoon minced onion*
1	*garlic clove, minced*
1/2	*teaspoon Worcestershire sauce*
3/4	*teaspoon salt*
1/4	*teaspoon pepper*
4	*cups water*
2	*tablespoons cornstarch dissolved in 2 tablespoons cold water*

PREPARATION

- Brown the ground beef in a sauté pan over medium heat. Stir in the chiles, onion, garlic, Worcestershire sauce, salt and pepper. Stirring gradually, pour in the water, then stir in the cornstarch mixture.

- Bring to a boil, reduce the heat to a simmer and cook about 10 minutes, stirring occasionally.

NOTE: Florence uses this sauce in enchiladas and burritos. It freezes well.

• SIX CUPS •

TORTILLA SOUP

INGREDIENTS

Soup

1¹/₂	tablespoons olive oil
1	medium onion, chopped
1	red bell pepper, seeded and chopped
1	stalk celery, chopped
2	garlic cloves, minced
8	cups chicken stock
1¹/₂	tablespoons garlic salt
1¹/₂	tablespoons ground white pepper
5	corn tortillas, roughly torn

Condiments

Thin strips of fried corn tortillas

Cooked diced chicken

Diced tomato

Diced green onions

Diced avocado

Grated Jack cheese

Sour cream

Cilantro sprigs

PREPARATION

■ Heat oil in a large heavy pot. Add onion, pepper, celery and garlic; sauté 4 to 5 minutes or until soft. Add chicken stock, garlic salt and white pepper; simmer 45 minutes.

■ Remove pot from heat and add tortillas. Allow to sit for 30 minutes. Strain broth and discard solids.

■ Pile an assortment of condiments in 6 wide shallow soup bowls and ladle broth over the top.

• SIX SERVINGS •

DEBORAH MADISON

Deborah Madison is a food writer and chef who lives in
Santa Fe, New Mexico. She has been cooking and gardening for more
than twenty years. In 1979 she was the founding chef of Greens
restaurant, the celebrated vegetarian restaurant in San Francisco.
She is the author of two award-winning cookbooks, *The Greens Cookbook*
(Bantam 1986) and *The Savory Way* (Bantam 1990), which was
named the Cookbook of the Year by the International Association
of Culinary Professionals.

Deborah teaches cooking throughout the country, writes
for a number of major publications, serves on the Santa Fe Farmers'
Market board, and is active with the Chef's Collaborative: 2000.
In 1995 she was awarded the MFK Fisher Mid-Career Award
by Les Dames Escoffier.

Chilled Tomato & Avocado Soup

Toasted Cheese Sandwiches with Mustard & Cumin

Poached Peaches & Raspberries

CHILLED TOMATO & AVOCADO SOUP

INGREDIENTS

4	cups chilled tomato juice
1/2	cup cilantro leaves, chopped
1	small garlic clove, finely chopped
2	green onions, finely chopped
1/2	jalapeño pepper, finely chopped
	juice of 1 large lime
1/4	teaspoon ground cumin
1	avocado, halved and pitted
4	thin lime slices
	cilantro leaves for garnish

PREPARATION

■ Pour the chilled tomato juice into a bowl or tureen. Stir in the cilantro, garlic, green onions, jalapeño pepper, lime juice, cumin and chopped avocado. Season to taste with salt and adjust other flavors to taste, adding more lime juice and cumin if desired.

■ Serve the soup cold, garnished with lime slices and cilantro leaves.

• FOUR SERVINGS •

TOASTED CHEESE SANDWICHES WITH MUSTARD & CUMIN

INGREDIENTS

4	slices light rye or whole wheat bread
1 1/3	cups shredded cheese, such as Jarlsberg, Swiss or Gruyère
4	teaspoons butter, softened
1	teaspoon Dijon mustard
1	teaspoon cumin seeds
	freshly ground black pepper

PREPARATION

■ Toast the bread on one side in a broiler or toaster oven. Work together the cheese, butter, mustard and cumin seeds until well blended; spread mixture on the untoasted sides of bread.

■ Broil until the cheese bubbles and starts to brown in spots. Grind on pepper. Cut sandwiches into halves on the diagonal and serve hot.

• FOUR SANDWICHES •

POACHED PEACHES & RASPBERRIES

. . . .

INGREDIENTS

1	*pint basket raspberries*
4	*peaches*
2/3	*cup water*
1/4	*cup sugar*
1	*small piece lemon peel*
	kirsch or rose water to taste
	almond cake or ice cream (optional)

PREPARATION

■ Mash 1/2 cup of the raspberries and force through a sieve to make about 2 tablespoons purée; set aside. Peel peaches by bringing a small pan of water to a boil, immersing the peaches for about 10 seconds, and then plunging them into cold water. Gently remove the skin with a knife and cut peaches into 3/4-inch thick wedges. Combine water, sugar and lemon peel in a medium saucepan and bring to a boil. When the sugar is dissolved, lower the heat, add the peaches and gently cook 2 to 5 minutes, until tender. With a slotted spoon, ladle cooked peaches into a serving bowl.

■ Bring syrup back to a boil and boil briskly 1 minute, then pour through a strainer into another bowl. Stir in raspberry purée and flavor with kirsch or rose water to taste. Pour hot raspberry syrup over peaches and add remaining raspberries, gently turning them in the syrup to coat. Cover and refrigerate until chilled. Serve with almond cake or scoops of ice cream, if desired.

• SIX SERVINGS •

Atlanta 1996

DONNA NORDIN

Donna Nordin, an influential chef in contemporary
Southwestern cooking in Arizona, was once mainly associated with
French cuisine in the San Francisco Bay area. For years she had
her own cooking school, La Grande Bouffe, and taught cooking classes
across the country.

In the early 1980s Donna moved to Tucson, Arizona, and in
1986 opened Café Terra Cotta. It continues to be the most popular
restaurant in Tucson today. In 1992 Donna and her husband opened
Café Terra Cotta in Scottsdale, Arizona, and most recently they
opened Trio Bistro/Bar in Tucson.

In 1994 Donna was inducted into the Arizona Culinary
Hall of Fame. Her cookbook, *Contemporary Southwest, the Café
Terra Cotta Cookbook*, was published in 1995.

Chile Slaw

---

*Beef Tenderloin on Roast Tomatillo Sauce with
Corn Salsa, Grilled Scallions & Portabellos*

Cold Lemon Soufflé

CHILE SLAW

· · · · · · · · · · · · · · · · · ·

INGREDIENTS

3	*poblano chiles, seeded and cut into very thin strips*
2	*red bell peppers, seeded and cut into very thin strips*
2	*yellow bell peppers, seeded and cut into very thin strips*
2	*small carrots, pared, cut into 2-inch long thin matchstick pieces*
1	*medium jicama, pared, cut into 2-inch long thin matchstick pieces*
2	*serrano chiles, minced*
1	*bunch cilantro, coarsely chopped*
2	*tomatoes, peeled and seeded*
3	*garlic cloves, minced*
1/2	*teaspoon ground cumin*
1	*cup sour cream*
	salt and pepper

PREPARATION

- Combine poblano chiles, bell peppers, carrots, jicama, serrano chiles and cilantro in a mixing bowl.

- In a food processor, blend tomatoes, garlic, cumin and sour cream until smooth. Season with salt and pepper.

- Pour sour cream mixture over vegetables; toss to coat. Let stand 15 minutes before serving to allow flavors to marry.

NOTE: Donna serves this slaw as a side dish with grilled fish or chicken.

· SIX TO EIGHT SERVINGS ·

Atlanta 1996

BEEF TENDERLOIN ON ROAST TOMATILLO SAUCE WITH CORN SALSA, GRILLED SCALLIONS & PORTABELLOS

INGREDIENTS

Corn Salsa

6	ears corn
2	red bell pepper, seeded, diced
2	green chiles, such as Anaheim or Fresno, seeded, finely diced
1	red onion, finely diced
1	bunch cilantro, coarsely chopped
1	teaspoon lime juice
1	teaspoon minced garlic

Roast Tomatillo Sauce

15	tomatillos, husks removed
2	teaspoons olive oil
1	onion, diced
6	chipotle chiles, seeded
1/2	cup (or more) chicken stock
1	bunch cilantro

Beef Tenderloin Roast

	oil for frying
8	bluecorn tortillas, cut into strips
1	beef tenderloin roast, 2 to 2½ pounds
8	portabello mushrooms
16	green onions

PREPARATION

- *To prepare the corn salsa:* Cook corn in a pot of boiling salted water 3 minutes; plunge into a bowl of ice water to stop the cooking. Drain and slice corn from the cob. In a medium bowl, combine corn with remaining salsa ingredients; adjust flavors to taste.

- *To prepare the roast tomatillo sauce:* Heat a cast-iron skillet over medium-high heat. Add tomatillos and toast, turning frequently, until tomatillos are browned in spots. Remove and cool. Add oil to skillet; heat over medium heat. Add onion and sauté until translucent, about 5 minutes. Add tomatillos, chipotles and 1/2 cup stock. Simmer about 10 minutes over low heat. Transfer to a blender and add cilantro. Purée until smooth. If sauce is too thick to pour easily, add more stock. Season with salt and pepper. Keep warm.

- *To prepare the beef and assemble:* In a heavy sauté pan, heat 1 inch of oil; fry tortillas in batches until crisp; drain on paper towels. Grill beef on a covered grill 16 to 24 minutes until a meat thermometer inserted in the center almost registers 150°F for medium-rare. (Cook 160°F for medium, or 170°F for well done.) Turn halfway through cooking. Let stand 5 to 10 minutes before slicing. Brush mushrooms and green onions with oil; grill until tender. Season with salt and pepper. Slice mushrooms.

- Carve 24 slices of beef, each 1/4 to 3/8 inches thick. Spoon tomatillo sauce onto each of 8 warmed plates. Arrange a cluster of tortilla strips in the center. Place 3 slices of beef around the tortillas and sprinkle corn salsa over the entire plate. Arrange grilled scallions and slices of mushrooms around the beef.

NOTE: When choosing a beef tenderloin roast, purchase a center-cut piece or a piece cut from the thicker end, as it will grill more evenly. Test with a thermometer to find out if beef is done, and remove beef from the grill just before it reaches the desired temperature.

• EIGHT SERVINGS •

COLD LEMON SOUFFLE

. . . .

INGREDIENTS

12	to 14 ladyfingers, split
	finely grated zest and juice of 3 lemons
1	envelope unflavored gelatin
6	egg yolks
³/₄	cup sugar
2	cups heavy cream
6	egg whites
	whipped cream and mint leaves, for garnish

PREPARATION

■ Line a 10-inch springform pan with ladyfingers. In a small bowl, combine lemon zest, lemon juice and gelatin; set aside. Combine egg yolks and sugar in a metal bowl set over simmering, not boiling, water. Beat with a hand-held electric mixer until mixture reaches 140°F on a candy thermometer. Stir in lemon-gelatin mixture and bring to 140°F again. Set mixing bowl in a bowl of ice and allow mixture to cool.

■ Meanwhile, beat cream until soft peaks form. In a separate bowl, beat egg whites until stiff but not dry. Gently fold the cream and whites into the cooled yolk mixture. Pour mixture into lined springform pan. Freeze. Garnish with additional whipped cream and mint leaves, if desired.

• EIGHT TO TEN SERVINGS •

MONIQUE BARBEAU

Monique Barbeau, a native of Vancouver, British Columbia,
is the chef of Fullers in the Sheraton Seattle Hotel and Towers. Fullers
has been rated as one of the top restaurants in the country by
Condé Nast Traveler since Monique has taken charge of the kitchen.
In 1992 the restaurant was voted number one in Seattle by the
Zagat Survey of America's Top Restaurants.

Monique is a graduate of the Culinary Institute of America.
Previously she worked at three New York City four-star restaurants:
Le Bernadin, the Quilted Giraffe and Chanterelle. In 1994
she was named Best Chef, Northwest, by the James Beard Foundation.

Saffron Fish Soup with Garlic Croutons & Rouille

Chocolate Banana Croissant Bread Pudding

SAFFRON FISH SOUP WITH GARLIC CROUTONS & ROUILLE

INGREDIENTS

Rouille

3	red bell peppers
1½	cups torn crustless French bread
⅓	to ½ cup water
1	large shallot, chopped
1	garlic clove, minced
2	tablespoons chopped fresh basil
¼	to ½ cup extra-virgin olive oil
	cayenne pepper, salt and pepper to taste

Croutons

40	slices French baguette, about ¼ inch thick
	olive oil
4	garlic cloves, peeled

PREPARATION

■ *To prepare the rouille:* Roast bell peppers over an open flame or in a broiler until the skin is charred and blistered. Place peppers in a large plastic food storage bag; set aside 5 to 10 minutes. Peel blistered peppers; remove seeds and stem. Cut peppers into strips.

■ Combine bread with ⅓ to ½ cup water to moisten. Let stand 5 minutes, then squeeze bread dry; discard liquid.

■ In a blender or food processor, process bell peppers, soaked bread, shallot, garlic and basil until smooth. Gradually add oil until thick and thoroughly blended. Use enough oil to make the rouille the consistency of mayonnaise. Season with cayenne pepper, salt and pepper to taste.

■ *To prepare the croutons:* Heat oven to 350°F. Brush bread slices lightly with oil. Place on baking sheets. Toast in oven until golden brown. Rub with garlic cloves.

Atlanta 1996

Soup Base

2	tablespoons olive oil
1/2	onion, thinly sliced
1	celery stalk, thinly sliced
1	fennel bulb, thinly sliced
1	large leek, thinly sliced
1	cup dry white wine
8	cups fish stock
	herb sachet bag (see Note)
	pinch saffron
6	garlic cloves, sliced
2	cups canned whole tomatoes, seeded and finely chopped
2	tablespoons Pernod liqueur
	salt and pepper to taste

Fish Fillets

4	tablespoons olive oil
8	cups cubed firm-texture skinless fish fillets, 3 to 4 pounds
2	cups dry white wine
12	oil-cured black olives, pitted and cut into slices
8	fennel sprigs for garnish

■ *To prepare the soup base:* Heat oil in a large heavy pot over medium heat. Add onion, celery, fennel and leek; sauté about 5 minutes. Add wine and bring to a boil; boil until reduced by half. Add fish stock, sachet bag, saffron, garlic and tomatoes. Bring to a boil, reduce heat and simmer 30 to 40 minutes. Remove and discard sachet bag. Add liqueur and season with salt and pepper to taste.

■ *To prepare the fish and serve:* Heat 1 tablespoon oil in a large sauté pan over high heat. Quickly brown about 2 cups fish; remove and set aside. Repeat with remaining oil and fish, browning in batches. Add wine to the pan and bring to a simmer. Return fish to pan and gently simmer 3 to 5 minutes until fish is cooked through. Remove pan from heat.

■ Ladle hot soup base into 8 wide shallow soup bowls. Place a spoonful of rouille in the middle of each bowl. Remove fish from wine with a slotted spoon and arrange fish around the rouille. Garnish with slivered olives and fennel sprigs. Serve remaining rouille and croutons separately.

NOTE: Bundle the following in a square of cheesecloth and tie: 3 parsley sprigs, celery tops from 1 stalk; 1/2 teaspoon fennel seeds, 1 bay leaf, 1 crushed garlic clove and 1/2 teaspoon black peppercorns.

• EIGHT SERVINGS •

CHOCOLATE BANANA CROISSANT BREAD PUDDING

INGREDIENTS

2	*large eggs*
3	*large egg yolks*
5	*tablespoons unsweetened cocoa powder*
1¹/₂	*cups packed brown sugar*
2¹/₂	*cups milk*
1	*cup heavy cream*
	pinch salt
¹/₂	*vanilla bean, split, scraped, seeds reserved*
¹/₂	*teaspoon ground nutmeg*
¹/₂	*teaspoon ground cinnamon*
3	*tablespoons sugar*
¹/₂	*cup brandy*
3	*tablespoons butter*
4	*firm bananas*
1¹/₂	*tablespoons lemon juice*
4	*large croissants, cut into cubes*
	vanilla ice cream or lightly sweetened whipped cream

PREPARATION

- Heat oven to 375°F. In the top of a double boiler, whisk eggs until blended. Whisk in cocoa powder and brown sugar until blended, then milk and cream. Place the top of the double boiler over the bottom pan and heat mixture until warm. Stir in the salt, spices, sugar and brandy. Continue cooking and stirring until the mixture thickens enough to coat a spoon.

- Heat butter in a small skillet. Peel and slice bananas; sauté in butter just until they soften. Sprinkle with lemon juice. Combine the chocolate custard, croissants and bananas; spoon into a buttered 2¹/₂-quart baking dish. Place the baking dish in a large pan and pour in hot water to come halfway up the sides. Bake about 30 minutes until set. Serve warm with ice cream or whipped cream.

• EIGHT SERVINGS •

TOM DOUGLAS

Tom Douglas is the executive chef/owner of the Dahlia Lounge
and Etta's Seafood in Seattle, Washington. Since moving to
Seattle from his native state of Delaware, Tom has helped define the
Northwest style of cooking. With the proximity of Asia, Alaska, California
and Canada, Northwest cuisine is a cornucopia of cultural influences.

In 1989 Tom opened his own restaurant with his wife Jackie
in the heart of downtown Seattle. Today the Dahlia Lounge is one of
Seattle's premier Northwest restaurants. In February of 1995,
Tom opened Etta's Seafood near Seattle's historic Pike Place Market.

Black Bean Soup with Roasted Tomatillo Salsa

*Pan-Fried Catfish with Mr. Joe's Tomato Gravy
& Smoky Bacon*

Ruby Red Grapefruit & Tequila Sorbet

BLACK BEAN SOUP WITH ROASTED TOMATILLO SALSA

· ·

INGREDIENTS

1	*pound tomatillos*
2	*tablespoons extra-virgin olive oil*
2	*pasilla or Anaheim peppers*
1/2	*cup finely chopped red onion*
1/4	*cup chopped cilantro leaves*
2	*teaspoons finely chopped garlic*
2	*tablespoons lime juice*
1	*teaspoon chipoltle pepper purée*
2	*cups dried black beans*
8	*cups chicken stock*
1	*ham hock*
2	*tablespoons olive oil*
1	*each medium onion, carrot, and celery stalk, chopped*
1	*tablespoon finely chopped garlic*
2	*cups canned tomatoes*
2	*teaspoons tomato paste*
2	*teaspoons ground coriander*
2	*teaspoons cumin seeds, toasted and ground*
2	*teaspoons paprika*
1	*teaspoon cayenne*
3	*tablespoons lime juice*
1/4	*cup chopped cilantro*

PREPARATION

■ Heat a cast-iron skillet over medium-high heat. Lightly coat the husked tomatillos with oil and add to the pan; roast until softened and lightly charred. Chop coarsely, then remove to a bowl, leaving most of the liquid behind.

■ Roast chiles over an open flame or in an oven broiler until skins are dark and blistered. Place in a paper or plastic food storage bag; close top. Set aside 5 to 10 minutes. Peel blistered chiles. Under running water, skins remove easily. Cut in half; remove seeds and stem; finely chop and add to bowl. Stir in next 5 ingredients.

■ Place beans in a pot with chicken stock and ham hock wrapped in cheesecloth. (Tom doesn't soak the beans before cooking because he thinks they retain better color that way.) Bring to a simmer, cover and cook until beans are soft, 2 to 2 1/2 hours. Heat oil in a sauté pan over medium-low heat. Add onion, carrot and celery; slowly cook in olive oil until onions are golden and caramelized. Add garlic the last few minutes of cooking. Add onion mixture, drained chopped tomatoes, tomato paste and spices to beans. Simmer another hour. Remove ham hock.

■ When cool enough to handle, remove all the meat from the ham hock and chop finely. Reserve. Purée soup in batches in the bowl of a food processor. Add chopped meat to soup. Season with salt and pepper to taste and lime juice. Reheat soup if necessary. Stir in chopped cilantro. Ladle into soup bowls and serve with dollops of the salsa. Garnish with sour cream.

NOTE: The roasted tomatillo salsa makes a lot more than you need to garnish the soup, but it is also delicious spooned over grilled fish or eaten with chips.

· EIGHT SERVINGS ·

PAN-FRIED CATFISH WITH MR. JOE'S TOMATO GRAVY & SMOKY BACON

. . . .

INGREDIENTS

Spice Rub

3	tablespoons paprika
1½	teaspoons cayenne
1	teaspoon dried thyme leaves
1	tablespoon salt
1	teaspoon freshly ground black pepper

Pan-Fried Catfish

8	slices bacon
⅔	cup chopped onion
1½	cups canned drained tomatoes
½	cup tomato sauce
2	teaspoons hot pepper sauce
	salt and pepper
2	teaspoons sugar
1	teaspoon cornstarch dissolved in 1 tablespoon cold water
4	(6-ounce) catfish fillets
3	tablespoons olive oil, or as needed for pan frying
	lemon wedges and chopped parsley for garnish

PREPARATION

- *To prepare the spice rub:* Combine paprika, cayenne, dried thyme leaves, salt and black pepper.

- *To prepare the catfish and serve:* Fry bacon crisp; set aside. Reserve 2 tablespoons fat and discard the rest. Sauté onion over medium-low heat in bacon fat until soft. Add tomatoes and tomato sauce; simmer 15 to 20 minutes. Remove sauce from pan and purée in a food processor. Return to pan and season with hot pepper sauce, salt, pepper and sugar. Add the dissolved cornstarch mixture to the sauce and simmer another 5 to 10 minutes, stirring frequently. Keep warm.

- Heat oven to 450°F. Pat 2 or 3 teaspoons of spice rub evenly over both sides of each catfish fillet. Heat oil in a large ovenproof sauté pan over medium-high heat. Panfry catfish on both sides until golden. Place the sauté pan in the oven until fish are just cooked through, about 5 to 7 minutes. While the catfish is cooking, heat the bacon by placing them in a pan in the oven for a few minutes.

- Ladle some of the Mr. Joe's gravy onto each of 4 plates. Place a catfish fillet over the gravy on each plate. Top each fillet with 2 slices of bacon. Garnish with lemon wedges and chopped parsley.

• FOUR SERVINGS •

RUBY RED GRAPEFRUIT & TEQUILA SORBET

. . . .

INGREDIENTS

Simple Syrup

$1/2$	cup water
$1/2$	cup sugar

Tequila Sorbet

5	cups freshly squeezed grapefruit juice, from Texas Ruby Reds or any pink grapefruit
$1/3$	cup tequila
2	tablespoons Grand Marnier liqueur
	lime wedges and mint sprigs for garnish
	crisp butter cookies

PREPARATION

- *To prepare the simple syrup:* Combine water and sugar in a small saucepan; heat, stirring until sugar dissolves. Cool and refrigerate to chill.

- *To prepare the sorbet:* Combine grapefruit juice, $3/4$ cup of the simple syrup, tequila and Grand Marnier in a large bowl; refrigerate to chill.

- Freeze in an ice cream maker following manufacturer's directions. Garnish sorbet with lime wedges and mint sprigs and serve with butter cookies.

NOTE: Tom serves the sorbet in chilled martini glasses. Dip the rims of the glasses in lime juice and then in sugar to give a "margarita" effect.

• ONE AND ONE-HALF QUARTS •

CORY SCHREIBER

Cory Schreiber, a fifth-generation Oregonian, started in the restaurant business at age eleven, first working for his family's famous restaurant, the Dan & Louis Oyster Bar in Portland. In 1994, Cory returned to hometown Portland to open his own restaurant, Wildwood, after having earned his culinary stars working with well-known restaurateurs and master chefs all over the country.

Schreiber's food is decidedly American with a Northwest bent. Wildwood's market-driven menus feature fresh seasonal ingredients utilizing local farms and purveyors—a diversity of meats, seafood, pizzas, pastas, vegetables, salads and savories.

Roasted Sweet Onion with Bacon, Frisée & Parmesan

Braised Pork with White Beans, Kale &
Winter Tomatoes

Sweet Potato Hazelnut Pound Cake

ROASTED SWEET ONION WITH BACON, FRISEE & PARMESAN

INGREDIENTS

4	*slices smoked bacon, cut in ¹/₂ inch pieces*
8	*garlic cloves, peeled*
2	*tablespoons olive oil*
1	*fennel bulb, cut and separated into long thin strips*
1	*red bell pepper, cored and cut into long thin strips*
1	*tablespoon finely chopped fresh thyme*
	salt and pepper
2	*tablespoons sherry vinegar or white wine vinegar*
3	*small white onions, peeled, cut in half crosswise*
	frisée lettuce
¹/₄	*cup finely grated Parmesan cheese*

PREPARATION

■ Heat oven to 350°F. In a large sauté pan over medium heat, render bacon until half cooked. Pour off fat. Add whole garlic cloves, olive oil, fennel strips, red pepper strips and thyme. Season with salt and pepper. Cook, stirring continually, 2 minutes. Add vinegar and cook another 1 to 2 minutes.

■ Place 6 approximately 8-inch squares of aluminum foil on a work surface. Place an onion half cut side up in the center of each piece of foil. Spoon fennel-red pepper mixture over onions, dividing evenly. Wrap up tightly and place packets on a baking sheet. Bake 45 minutes or until onions are tender.

■ Place a small handful of frisée lettuce on each of 6 salad plates. Unwrap foil packets and arrange vegetables and any juices from the packet over frisée. Sprinkle with Parmesan cheese.

• SIX SERVINGS •

Atlanta 1996

BRAISED PORK WITH WHITE BEANS, KALE & WINTER TOMATOES

. . . .

INGREDIENTS

2	cups small dried white beans
2	tablespoons plus ¼ cup olive oil, divided
1	boneless pork shoulder roast
	salt and pepper
2	carrots, coarsely chopped
2	white onions, coarsely chopped
1	stalk celery, coarsely chopped
¼	cup balsamic vinegar
1	can (16 ounces) stewed tomatoes
½	cup tomato paste
8	cups chicken stock
2	whole bulbs garlic, cut in half, plus 4 minced garlic cloves
1	tablespoon chopped fresh thyme
1	bunch kale, leaves torn into bite-size pieces

PREPARATION

■ Cover beans with water and soak overnight; drain. Place beans in a pot, cover with salted water and cook about 1 hour until tender. Set aside.

■ Heat oven to 350°F. Heat 2 tablespoons oil in a large ovenproof casserole over medium-high heat. Season pork with salt and pepper; brown both sides in hot oil. Remove pork from pan; pour off all but a few teaspoons of fat. Add carrots, onions and celery; cook, stirring frequently, until vegetables brown. Add vinegar and cook, stirring, about 1 minute.

■ Drain and reserve juice from stewed tomatoes; coarsely chop tomatoes and set aside. Add drained juice, tomato paste, chicken stock, garlic bulbs and thyme to pan. Bring liquid to a simmer and add pork shoulder. Place casserole in oven, uncovered, and cook, turning pork several times, for 1½ to 2 hours until pork is very tender. Remove pork from casserole; place casserole with braising juices on the stove top over high heat. Boil to reduce to 4 cups; strain.

■ In a large sauté pan, heat remaining ¼ cup olive oil over medium heat. Add kale and sauté 1 minute. Add 4 minced garlic cloves, reserved stewed tomatoes and white beans. Add strained braising liquid and simmer about 5 minutes until kale wilts. Season with salt and pepper.

■ To serve, slice pork and place in wide shallow bowls. Spoon bean mixture with broth over the top.

• SIX TO EIGHT SERVINGS •

SWEET POTATO HAZELNUT POUND CAKE

. . . .

INGREDIENTS

1	*large sweet potato*
1³/₄	*cups all-purpose flour*
¹/₂	*teaspoon baking powder*
¹/₂	*teaspoon salt*
¹/₂	*teaspoon ground cinnamon*
¹/₂	*teaspoon ground nutmeg*
³/₄	*cup unsalted butter, softened*
1¹/₂	*cups sugar*
3	*large eggs*
1	*teaspoon vanilla extract*
¹/₂	*cup buttermilk*
2	*tablespoons water*
¹/₂	*cup hazelnuts, toasted, skins rubbed off, chopped*
	lightly sweetened whipped cream, if desired

PREPARATION

■ The day before the cake is to be made, bake the sweet potato in a 350°F. oven 50 to 60 minutes until soft. When cooked, peel off the skin and place the flesh in a strainer set over a bowl. Let drain overnight. Purée the flesh or mash with a fork to make 1 cup purée.

■ Butter a 10-inch layer cake pan. Heat oven to 350°F. Sift together flour, baking powder, salt and spices. In a large bowl with electric beaters, beat butter and sugar until light and fluffy. Continue beating, adding 1 egg at a time until thoroughly blended. Beat in vanilla. Gently mix in dry ingredients alternately with buttermilk and water, beginning and ending with dry ingredients. Add sweet potato purée and hazelnuts; mix just to blend. Spread batter into prepared pan.

■ Bake 30 to 35 minutes until a wooden pick inserted in the center comes out clean. Cool cake in pan 15 minutes then unmold. Serve wedges with whipped cream, if desired.

• TWELVE SERVINGS •

Atlanta 1996

ALAN WONG

Alan Wong is chef/owner of Alan Wong's Restaurant in
Honolulu, Hawaii. The restaurant specializes in regional Hawaiian cuisine,
a blend of island ingredients with an Asian twist.

Alan earned his cooking stripes at the famed Lutece restaurant in
New York City and the Mauna Lani Bay Hotel in Honolulu.
He has been recognized by the James Beard Foundation as Best Chef,
Northwest, and in 1994 received the Robert Mondavi Culinary
Award of Excellence.

Ahi Poki Salad with Lemon Grass Chili Dressing

*Ribs with Hoisin Barbecue Sauce
& Tropical Fruit Relish*

Hawaiian Chocolate Mousse

AHI POKI SALAD WITH
LEMON GRASS CHILI DRESSING

. . . .

INGREDIENTS

Lemon Grass Chili Dressing

1/4	cup lime juice
1/4	cup soy sauce
1/4	cup water
1/4	cup sugar
1	tablespoon fish sauce
2	teaspoons sambal chili sauce
2	tablespoons minced lemon grass
1	tablespoon minced fresh ginger
2	teaspoons minced garlic

Ahi Poki Salad

2 1/2	cups cubed fresh raw ahi tuna
1/2	cup finely diced white onion
1/3	cup thinly sliced green onions
3	tablespoons sambal oleke*
3/4	teaspoon inamona*
1	tablespoon sesame oil
	salt to taste
6	cups mixed field greens

* Available at some specialty food stores
  and by mail order.

PREPARATION

■ *To prepare the dressing:* Mix together lime juice, soy sauce, water, sugar, fish sauce, chili sauce, lemon grass, ginger and garlic, stirring until sugar dissolves.

■ *To prepare the salad:* In a mixing bowl, toss together tuna, onion, green onions, sambal oleke, inamona and sesame oil. Season to taste with salt. Toss greens with dressing to coat; arrange on 6 salad plates. Top with tuna.

• SIX SERVINGS •

RIBS WITH HOISIN BARBECUE SAUCE & TROPICAL FRUIT RELISH

• • • • • • • • • • • • • • • • • • •

INGREDIENTS

Tropical Fruit Relish

1	cup diced pineapple
1	cup diced papaya
1/2	cup seeded diced tomato
1/4	cup thinly sliced green onions
2	tablespoons chopped fresh mint
2	tablespoons seasoned rice vinegar

Pork Ribs

2	tablespoons Chinese black beans
3/4	cup hoisin sauce
1/2	cup honey
5	tablespoons dark soy sauce
5	tablespoons dry sherry
3	tablespoons sesame oil
3	tablespoons curry powder
1	tablespoon chili sauce
1	cup ketchup
1/3	cup white vinegar
1/4	cup sesame seeds, toasted
2	tablespoons finely grated orange zest
2	teaspoons minced garlic
5	to 6 pounds pork loin back ribs

PREPARATION

- *To prepare the fruit relish:* Combine pineapple, papaya, tomato, green onions, mint and vinegar in a bowl; set aside.

- *To prepare the ribs and serve:* Soak black beans in water for 10 minutes. Rinse and chop. Combine black beans with hoisin sauce, honey, soy sauce, sherry, oil, curry powder, chili sauce, ketchup, vinegar, sesame seeds, orange zest and garlic and mix well.

- Grill ribs on a covered gas or charcoal grill 8 to 12 minutes, turning and rearranging ribs frequently. Brush ribs with sauce the last 4 or 5 minutes of cooking. Remove ribs from grill and baste with sauce. Serve with additional sauce and fruit relish.

• SIX SERVINGS •

Atlanta 1996

HAWAIIAN CHOCOLATE MOUSSE

INGREDIENTS

1	*cup Hawaiian Vintage Chocolate pistoles or other good quality chocolate pieces*
2	*cups whipping cream*
1	*to 2 tablespoons Hawaiian macadamia nut liqueur*
¼	*cup chopped, toasted macadamia nuts*

PREPARATION

■ Melt chocolate in a mixing bowl set over water in a saucepan set over low heat. Pour about ¹/₂ cup cream into melted chocolate, stirring to make a smooth paste. Add more cream slowly and stir until smooth. Keep adding cream in small amounts until it's all incorporated. Remove from heat.

■ With electric beaters, beat chocolate cream until mixture thickens and holds its shape. Fold in liqueur and nuts. Spoon mousse into stemmed glasses and refrigerate to chill and set.

NOTE: Alan also refrigerates this mousse in the mixing bowl until it's set and then scoops it out onto dessert plates and surrounds with fresh fruit.

• SIX SERVINGS •

Atlanta 1996

ROY YAMAGUCHI

Chef and restaurateur Roy Yamaguchi has become a leader
in revitalizing an Hawaiian regional cuisine. After graduating from high
school in Tokyo, Japan, Roy enrolled in the Culinary Institute
of New York. He spent his first professional years in three of Los Angeles's
finest French kitchens. His work ethic and talent earned him
a "boy wonder" reputation.

In 1984 Roy created his own restaurant, 385 North, in West Hollywood,
where his highly personal "Euro-Asian" style came into bloom.
Despite his success in southern California, Roy yearned for another life in
the homeland of his father and grandparents, the Hawaiian Islands.
In 1988 he opened the first Roy's Restaurant. Since then he has
opened six more, including three in the Hawaiian Islands, and one each
in Tokyo, Guam, and Pebble Beach, California.

In addition to receiving numerous awards and accolades, Roy
has just completed a second season of his Hawaii Public Television series,
"Hawaii Cooks with Roy Yamaguchi."

*Blackened Island Ahi
with Soy Mustard Butter Sauce*

Macadamia Nut Bread

BLACKENED ISLAND AHI WITH SOY MUSTARD BUTTER SAUCE

· · · · · · · · · · · · · · · · · · · ·

INGREDIENTS

Mustard Soy Sauce

$^1/_4$	cup Coleman's dry mustard
2	tablespoons hot water
2	tablespoons rice wine vinegar
$^1/_4$	cup soy sauce

White Butter Sauce

1	cup white wine
2	teaspoons white wine vinegar
$1^1/_2$	teaspoons minced shallot
$^1/_2$	cup heavy cream
$^1/_2$	cup (1 stick) chilled unsalted butter, diced into small cubes

Tuna

$1^1/_2$	tablespoons paprika
$^1/_2$	teaspoon cayenne pepper
$^1/_2$	teaspoon red chile powder
$^1/_4$	teaspoon ground white pepper
$^1/_2$	tablespoon ground sandalwood
2	ahi tuna fillets, about 7 ounces each, cut in half lengthwise

Garnish

	spice sprouts, top 2 inches only
	pickled ginger
$^1/_2$	teaspoon black sesame seeds

PREPARATION

- *To prepare the mustard soy sauce:* In a small bowl, stir together the mustard and hot water to form a paste. Let sit a few minutes for the flavor and heat to develop. Stir in the vinegar and soy sauce. Strain the sauce through a fine sieve. Refrigerate to chill.

- *To prepare the white butter sauce:* Bring the wine, wine vinegar and shallot to a boil in a medium saucepan over medium-high heat. Boil to reduce to $^1/_2$ cup. Add the cream and continue to boil to reduce to $^1/_3$ cup. Reduce the heat to low and gradually add pieces of butter, stirring slowly (do not whisk) until all of the butter is incorporated. Be careful not to let the mixture boil, or it will break and separate. Season to taste with salt and white pepper. Strain through a fine sieve. Transfer the sauce to the top of a double boiler set over hot water to keep the sauce warm.

- *To prepare the tuna:* Mix all the spices together in a shallow dish, such as a pie plate. Press 1 side of each piece of tuna into the spice mixture to coat. Lightly oil and heat a cast-iron skillet over high heat. Quickly sear the tuna over high heat to the desired doneness (about 45 seconds per side for rare; 1 minute for medium-rare.)

- *To assemble:* Spoon the mustard soy sauce over half of a serving plate and sauce the other half of the dish with the white butter sauce. Place the ahi in the middle and garnish with spice sprouts, pickled ginger and sesame seeds.

NOTE: May substitute sunflower sprouts for spice sprouts.

· FOUR SERVINGS ·

MACADAMIA NUT BREAD

· ·

INGREDIENTS

¹/₂	cup unsalted butter (1 stick), at room temperature
³/₄	cup granulated sugar
¹/₂	cup brown sugar
1	pound over-ripe bananas
3¹/₃	cups all-purpose flour
2	teaspoons baking powder
2	teaspoons baking soda
2	large eggs
¹/₃	cup water
¹/₂	cup macadamia nuts, chopped
¹/₄	cup raisins
¹/₄	cup shredded coconut

PREPARATION

■ Heat oven to 350°F. Grease and flour a deep 9-inch round layer cake pan, springform pan or a loaf pan. In the bowl of an electric mixer, beat the butter and both sugars until creamy and smooth. Peel and mash the bananas with a fork. Add the bananas to the butter mixture and mix 1 minute.

■ Sift together the flour, baking powder and baking soda; gradually add to the butter mixture, beating until well blended. Add the eggs and water; continue to beat for 1 minute. Reserve 2 tablespoons chopped macadamia nuts for the top. Stir the remaining macadamia nuts, raisins and coconut into the batter.

■ Scrape the batter into the prepared pan. Sprinkle the top with the reserved macadamia nuts. Bake 35 to 45 minutes until a wooden pick inserted in the center comes out clean. Remove to a wire rack to cool.

· EIGHT TO TEN SERVINGS ·

MICHAEL CHIARELLO

Michael Chiarello, chef of Tra Vigne Restaurant in St. Helena, California, grew up in a family devoted to its Italian heritage of good food. As a child, in central California, Michael lived in a style close to his family's Calabrian roots in southern Italy. His grandmother baked bread in an outdoor clay oven and gathered vegetables for meals from her garden. Food—its growing, preparing, cooking, and preserving—was the center of family life.

In 1986 Michael opened Tra Vigne, Italian for "among the vines." The restaurant produces many of its ingredients on the premises, including prosciutto, braesola, salami, various cheeses and cured olives. He spends half his creative time on ingredients because, he says, eighty-five percent of the results depends on their integrity.

In addition to his responsibilities as a chef, Michael is one of the founders of Consorzio Foods, which produces some of his signature, Italian-inspired ingredients for commercial sale. His new ventures include ownership in Ajax Tavern and Bumps, both in Aspen, Colorado, and the Caffé Museo in the new San Francisco Museum of Modern Art.

Pastina Autunna

Garlic Crab

Budino di Cioccolata

PASTINA AUTUNNA

. . . .

INGREDIENTS

Mushroom Stock

3	cups wild mushrooms, such as chanterelles, porcini or oyster mushrooms
3	cups white mushrooms, sliced
1½	quarts chicken stock

Pasta & Sauce

¼	cup diced pancetta or bacon
¼	cup olive oil
10	tablespoons butter, divided
1½	cups diced carrots, in ¼-inch pieces
	salt and pepper
2	tablespoons chopped garlic
2	tablespoons chopped thyme
¾	cup heavy cream
1	pound pastina, preferably acini di pepe
12	brussels sprouts, cored and leaves separated
¾	cup balsamic vinegar
1	cup finely grated Parmesan cheese, plus additional for the top

PREPARATION

■ *To make the mushroom stock:* Remove stems from wild mushrooms; reserve tops for sauce. Place wild mushroom stems, sliced white mushrooms and stock in a large saucepan. Bring to a boil, reduce heat and simmer gently 1 hour. Strain through a fine mesh sieve.

■ *To make the sauce:* Heat a large heavy sauté pan over medium-high heat. Add the pancetta and cook until almost crisp. Remove pancetta and reserve. Pour off fat. In the same pan, heat the olive oil and 2 tablespoons butter over medium-high heat. Add the carrots and cook 3 to 5 minutes or until they start to lightly brown and caramelize. Slice the wild mushroom tops reserved from the mushroom stock. Add to the pan and cook 3 to 4 minutes, tossing occasionally until the mushrooms are browned. Season with salt and pepper. Add the pancetta and increase the heat. Cook for 1 to 2 minutes. Add the garlic and cook another 1 or 2 minutes. Add the thyme, mushroom stock and cream. Bring to a boil and cook until reduced by about a third.

■ Meanwhile, cook the pastina in boiling salted water until it is slightly undercooked (it will be finished in the sauce). Add the pastina and brussels sprouts to the sauce. Remove saucepan from the heat, add remaining butter and cheese and stir until fully incorporated.

■ Pour 2 tablespoons balsamic vinegar onto each serving plate. Spoon the pasta over the vinegar. Top with additional cheese.

• SIX SERVINGS •

GARLIC CRAB

INGREDIENTS

4	*Dungeness crabs, cleaned*
6	*tablespoons butter*
6	*tablespoons olive oil*
2	*tablespoons minced garlic*
1/4	*cup minced parsley*
3	*tablespoons lemon juice*

PREPARATION

■ Heat oven to the hottest possible temperature, 475° to 500°F. Place the crab in 1 layer in a roasting pan. Heat the butter, olive oil and garlic in a small saucepan until butter has melted. Season with salt and pepper.

■ Pour butter mixture over crab and roast in the oven 10 to 15 minutes until garlic turns a light brown. Remove crab from the oven; sprinkle with parsley and lemon juice.

• FOUR SERVINGS •

BUDINO DI CIOCCOLATA

INGREDIENTS

1/4	*cup (1/2 stick) sweet butter*
8	*ounces bittersweet or semisweet chocolate*
	finely grated zest of 1 lemon
3	*egg yolks*
1/2	*cup sugar, divided*
1/4	*cup espresso*
1/4	*cup sifted chestnut flour*
3	*egg whites*
	lightly sweetened whipped cream

PREPARATION

■ Heat oven to 475° to 500°F. In a small saucepan over medium-high heat, heat butter until melted; cook until butter just starts to brown. Remove from heat and let stand for 1 or 2 minutes; add chocolate and stir until melted. Stir in lemon zest.

■ In a mixer bowl, beat egg yolks and 1/4 cup sugar until thick and pale yellow. Stir in chocolate mixture and espresso until well blended. Fold in chestnut flour. In a separate bowl, beat egg whites until softly whipped. Gradually add sugar and beat until stiff. Fold into batter.

■ Spoon into six 8-ounce soufflé dishes. Bake about 8 minutes until the outside of the dessert becomes cake-like but the center remains the consistency of pudding. Serve warm with whipped cream.

NOTE: At the restaurant, Michael serves this dessert with roasted chestnut syrup and sour cherry zabaglione.

• SIX SERVINGS •

Atlanta 1996

FRED HALPERT

Chef/proprietor Fred Halpert features what he calls "cuisines of the sun" at his wine country bistro, Brava Terrace, in California's Napa Valley. Inspired by the wine country cooking of France and Italy, Fred honed his skills under the tutelage of some of Europe's finest chefs. After returning to the United States he was attracted to California's restaurant revolution and in 1990 opened Brava Terrace just north of St. Helena.

Brava Terrace boasts a lush, outdoor terrace with priceless views of vineyards, hills and blue skies. Fred selects all the wines on the wine list to complement his cooking style. Out back he plants an organic garden of herbs, tomatoes and vegetables.

Salmon Salad with Sun-Dried Tomato Vinaigrette

Roasted Breast of Chicken with Fava Beans, Grilled Portabello Mushrooms & Tarragon

Risotto with Pistachio Pesto

SALMON SALAD WITH SUN-DRIED TOMATO VINAIGRETTE

. . . .

INGREDIENTS

¹/₂	**cup dry red wine**
6	**to 8 sun-dried tomato halves**
1	**pound salmon fillets**
¹/₄	**cup plus 1 tablespoon olive oil, divided**
2	**teaspoons balsamic vinegar**
2	**teaspoons lemon juice**
2	**shallots, finely chopped**
	salt and ground white pepper
6	**to 8 cups assorted bite-size salad greens**
3	**tablespoons chopped mixed fresh herbs such as basil, chives, dill and chervil**

PREPARATION

■ Heat wine in a small saucepan over medium heat. Add tomatoes, remove pan from heat and let stand until cooled. Drain and cut tomatoes into slivers; set aside. Slice salmon fillets thinly on the bias into 8 equal pieces; set aside.

■ In a small bowl, whisk together ¹/₄ cup olive oil, vinegar, lemon juice and shallots; season to taste with salt and white pepper. Toss together salad greens and slivered tomatoes with dressing and half the herbs; pile onto 8 salad plates.

■ Heat remaining 1 tablespoon oil in a large heavy sauté pan over high heat. Season the salmon with salt and pepper, then sauté quickly, just to brown lightly on both sides. Arrange salmon on greens and sprinkle with remaining herbs.

• EIGHT SERVINGS •

ROASTED BREAST OF CHICKEN WITH FAVA BEANS, GRILLED PORTABELLO MUSHROOMS & TARRAGON

INGREDIENTS

8	*boneless chicken breasts*
4	*medium carrots, medium diced*
4	*celery stalks, medium diced*
2	*onions, medium diced*
4	*cloves garlic, minced*
4	*sprigs fresh thyme*
$^1/_2$	*pound Yukon Gold potatoes*
$^1/_4$	*cup ($^1/_2$ stick) butter*
$^1/_4$	*cup finely chopped shallots, divided*
	salt and pepper
4	*tablespoons olive oil, divided*
$^1/_2$	*pound Fava beans, shelled*
6	*ounces Portabello mushrooms*
$^1/_2$	*small bunch tarragon, leaves chopped*

PREPARATION

■ Heat oven to 450°F. Debone chicken breasts; place bones in a roasting pan. Roast bones until lightly browned. Add carrots, celery, onions, garlic and thyme; roast about 1 hour longer, stirring occasionally. Remove pan from oven and place contents in a large pot. Cover with water and simmer until reduced by $^2/_3$. Strain broth and set aside.

■ Slice potatoes crosswise into $^1/_4$-inch thick slices. Heat butter in a large heavy sauté pan over medium heat. Add half the shallots and the sliced potatoes; sauté until potatoes are browned and tender. Season with salt and pepper.

■ In a separate pan, heat 1 tablespoon olive oil. Sauté remaining shallots and fava beans in some of the olive oil; season with salt and pepper.

■ Brush mushrooms with remaining olive oil and grill over gas or charcoal until browned and tender; season with salt and pepper. Slice mushrooms and combine with potatoes and fava beans. Sprinkle with tarragon and place vegetables in the middle of serving plates. Season chicken breasts and grill just until cooked through.

■ Place chicken on top of vegetables. Meanwhile, reheat reduced chicken broth, season accordingly, and spoon some of it over the chicken and vegetables.

• EIGHT SERVINGS •

Atlanta 1996

RISOTTO WITH PISTACHIO PESTO

· ·

INGREDIENTS

Pesto

¹/₂	cup shelled pistachios
3	bunches fresh basil
4	garlic cloves, peeled
¹/₃	cup extra-virgin olive oil
¹/₄	cup grated asiago cheese
	salt and pepper

Risotto

¹/₄	cup olive oil
2	white onions, quartered
5	garlic cloves, finely chopped
2	sprigs thyme, leaves chopped
2	sprigs rosemary, leaves chopped
2	sprigs basil, leaves chopped
2	cups arborio rice
2¹/₂	cups chicken stock
1	cup water
¹/₂	cup finely grated Parmesan cheese
	salt and pepper

PREPARATION

■ *To prepare the pesto:* Heat oven to 350°F. Place pistachios on a baking sheet and roast 5 to 8 minutes until lightly browned. Cool and then coarsely chop; set aside less than a quarter of the pistachios for garnish.

■ In a food processor, process the remaining pistachios, basil leaves and garlic cloves until finely chopped. With the machine running, slowly add the olive oil; process to a paste. Add the cheese and process until incorporated. Season the mixture with salt and pepper; set aside.

■ *To prepare the risotto:* Heat the olive oil in a large saucepan over medium-high heat. Add the onions, garlic, thyme, rosemary and basil; sauté until onions are lightly brown. Add rice; sauté another 1 or 2 minutes.

■ Combine the chicken stock and water in a separate saucepan and bring to a boil. Slowly add 1 cup of the hot liquid to the rice, stirring constantly. When the liquid has been absorbed, add ¹/₂ cup more and allow it to simmer, stirring well until it has been absorbed. Continue cooking, adding liquid ¹/₂ cup at a time and stirring constantly until the rice is slightly creamy and just tender. Stir in the pesto and then ²/₃ of the cheese. Season with salt and pepper.

■ Serve in wide shallow bowls. Top with remaining cheese and chopped pistachios.

· EIGHT SERVINGS ·

Atlanta 1996

REED HEARON

Reed Hearon is one of the busiest and most successful chefs
in the country today. In just a few years he's launched three acclaimed
restaurants and two cookbooks. Reed's restaurants LuLu and
LuLu Bis stand in the heart of San Francisco's Yerba Buena Arts District.
Restaurant LuLu's cuisine of the Riviera, dynamic interior and
lively crowd have earned rave reviews as well as a dynamic
local following. With Cafe Marimba, a very different restaurant located
in the Marina District of San Francisco, the chef returns to
his first love—authentic Mexican cuisine. The menu features
dishes from Oaxaca and the Yucatan.

Rattlesnake Salsa

*Salad of Raw Artichokes, Fava Beans
& Parmesan Cheese*

Iron Skillet Mussels

RATTLESNAKE SALSA

. . . .

INGREDIENTS

3	*cascabel chiles*
2	*garlic cloves, unpeeled*
1	*large tomato*
2	*tomatillos*
2	*tablespoons apple cider vinegar*
1/4	*teaspoon dried oregano leaves, preferably Mexican oregano*
	pinch ground cloves
1	*cup water*
1	*teaspoon olive oil*
1/4	*teaspoon salt*

PREPARATION

■ In a heavy skillet, such as a cast-iron skillet, over medium heat toast chiles until brown and fragrant, about 3 minutes. Remove chiles. Add unpeeled garlic; toast until browned and soft, then peel.

■ Bring 3 inches of water to a boil in a medium saucepan. Add tomato and husked tomatillos; reduce heat and simmer 3 to 5 minutes until soft. Remove tomatoes and tomatillos to a work surface; coarsely chop.

■ Place all ingredients in a food processor or blender; process to a slightly textured salsa. Adjust seasonings to taste.

• ABOUT TWO AND ONE-HALF CUPS •

SALAD OF RAW ARTICHOKES, FAVA BEANS & PARMESAN CHEESE

INGREDIENTS

2	*cups water*
	juice of 4 lemons
¼	*cup extra-virgin olive oil*
15	*baby artichokes*
1	*pound fava beans*
	salt and pepper
2	*ounces Parmesan cheese, thinly shaved with a vegetable peeler*

PREPARATION

■ Combine 2 cups of water and the juice of 3 of the lemons in a bowl. Combine the juice of the remaining lemon and the oil in another bowl. Strip the artichokes of their outer leaves and cut off the sharp points; discard. Immerse the artichokes in the lemon water.

■ Peel the fava beans of both their outer and inner husks; add to the lemon-oil mixture and toss to coat. Remove 1 artichoke at a time from the water and slice very thinly; quickly toss with lemon-oil mixture. Repeat with remaining artichokes. Season with salt and pepper. Serve salad topped with shaved Parmesan cheese.

NOTE: Raw artichokes quickly turn brown and bitter when their cut surfaces are exposed to air. To prevent this, work quickly and keep the artichokes immersed in lemon water or vinaigrette.

• FIVE TO SIX SERVINGS •

IRON SKILLET MUSSELS

INGREDIENTS

2	*pounds small mussels, debearded and scrubbed clean*
	salt and pepper
½	*cup clarified butter*

PREPARATION

■ Over high heat preheat a large cast-iron skillet or griddle until very hot, about 4 minutes. Place mussels directly on skillet, adding no other ingredients. In about 2 minutes they'll open.

■ When opened, remove mussels and sprinkle with salt and pepper. Serve with clarified butter.

NOTE: At the restaurant, Reed cooks a pound of mussels for each diner on a medium skillet and serves the mussels right on the skillet.

• FOUR APPETIZERS OR TWO MAIN DISH SERVINGS •

CHRISTOPHER KUMP & MARGARET FOX

Christopher Kump

Christopher Kump has been immersed in the world of food since his early years. From the age of eight, he spent summers in Europe with his father, Peter Kump, owner of Peter Kump's New York Cooking School. He also had the advantage of attending and assisting classes at his father's school, working with and learning from distinguished chefs and cookbook authors. In 1984 Chris answered a classified ad for a dinner chef placed by Cafe Beaujolais owner Margaret Fox. Today, Chris is executive chef for the restaurant and Margaret's husband and partner.

Margaret Fox

Successful restaurateur, chef and cookbook author Margaret Fox has come a long way from her first culinary triumphs with French toast and rice pudding at age nine. While other children were making mud pies, Margaret was baking alongside her mother, whose love for cooking was passed on to her daughter.

Margaret's desire for a tranquil pace led her to Mendocino, a picturesque coastal town 150 miles north of San Francisco, where she purchased Cafe Beaujolais in 1977. Margaret's magic with breakfasts and her wonderful desserts have won her accolades from food critics and writers across the country. She chronicles the joys and pitfalls of owning a country restaurant in her book *Cafe Beaujolais* and features her wonderful breakfast recipes in *Morning Food*.

Roasted Eggplant & Tapenade Tart

Grilled Figs, Chanterelles & Prosciutto on Arugula

Huckleberry Pie

ROASTED EGGPLANT & TAPENADE TART

INGREDIENTS

2	*Japanese eggplant*
2	*small heads garlic*
	olive oil
	salt and pepper
1	*large egg*
$^1/_2$	*cup milk*
$^1/_4$	*cup heavy cream*
	pinch ground allspice
1	*tablespoon chopped flat-leaf parsley*
1	*cup quality brine-cured black olives, pitted*
2	*anchovy fillets*
1	*tablespoon capers*
$^1/_2$	*teaspoon minced fresh thyme*
1	*tablespoon dark rum*
	baked 9-inch tart shell

PREPARATION

■ Heat the oven to 375°F. Pare 2 opposite long sides of the eggplant, then slice lengthwise to between $^1/_4$ and $^3/_8$ inch thick. (Slice eggplant parallel to the sides you peeled so there are no end pieces with all the skin on one side.) Break apart the heads of garlic; set aside 1 clove. Lightly oil a parchment-lined baking sheet. Arrange the eggplant in 1 layer on the baking sheet along with the remaining garlic cloves. Drizzle olive oil over the garlic and brush some on the eggplant; sprinkle lightly with salt. Roast about 20 minutes until the eggplants are golden brown and soft. If any pieces get too dark before all are done, remove them from the oven. Allow to cool slightly.

■ While still warm, squeeze the roasted garlic out of its skin directly into the bowl of a food processor. Peel the reserved raw garlic clove and add it to the bowl. Process until garlic is smooth. Add the egg, milk, cream and allspice; process to blend. Add the chopped parsley and pinch of salt. (The custard should be underseasoned at this point because it will be combined with saltier ingredients later.) Remove the mixture from the food processor and set aside.

■ In the same food processor bowl, process the olives, anchovies, capers, thyme and rum to make a paste. If the mixture seems dry, add a little olive oil.

■ Reduce the oven heat to 350°F. Spread the olive paste over the bottom of the tart shell. Layer the eggplant and custard in the shell in 3 layers, finishing with custard. Bake 30 minutes until the custard is set. Cool on a wire rack before slicing. Serve at room temperature.

• EIGHT SERVINGS •

GRILLED FIGS, CHANTERELLES & PROSCIUTTO ON ARUGULA

· · · · · · · · · · · · · · · · · ·

INGREDIENTS

6	*to 8 ounces chanterelle mushrooms*
10	*fresh Black Mission figs*
1/3	*cup balsamic vinegar*
2/3	*cup fruity olive oil*
	salt and ground black pepper
4	*ounces thinly sliced prosciutto*
2	*quarts, loosely packed, young arugula leaves*
1/4	*cup mixed edible flowers, such as nasturtium, borage and calendula petals (optional)*

PREPARATION

■ To clean the chanterelle mushrooms, do not immerse in water. First brush loose dirt away from the gills and caps with a vegetable or pastry brush, then wipe off any dirt remaining on the caps with a towel, and if necessary, use a knife to cut away any embedded grit. Cut the mushrooms into halves, quarters or large bite-size pieces depending on their size. Cut the figs into halves from stem to tail.

■ In a small bowl with a wire whisk, whisk together the vinegar and oil. Season lightly with salt and pepper. Set aside 6 tablespoons of the dressing. Toss the fig halves and chanterelles with the remaining dressing. Season generously with pepper and set aside to marinate for about 30 minutes, tossing once or twice.

■ Cut the prosciutto into 1x3-inch pieces. Wrap the figs with prosciutto strips. Cut any leftover prosciutto into smaller strips and set aside. Thread the prosciutto-wrapped figs on bamboo skewers alternately with the chanterelles. Add any leftover marinade to the 6 tablespoons set aside.

■ Grill the skewers over gas or charcoal in a covered grill 1 to 2 minutes per side until lightly browned. Toss the arugula and reserved dressing to coat; divide among 4 salad plates. Remove the figs and mushrooms from the skewers and arrange over the arugula. Intersperse with reserved prosciutto trimmings. Sprinkle with edible flowers, if desired.

· FIVE SERVINGS ·

Atlanta 1996

HUCKLEBERRY PIE

. . . .

INGREDIENTS

5	cups huckleberries, fresh or frozen
$1/3$	to $1/2$ cup sugar or to taste depending on the tartness of berries
$1/4$	cup quick-cooking tapioca
	baked 9-inch pie shell
	pie dough for lattice topping
1	egg, lightly beaten
2	tablespoons unsalted butter, cut in small pieces
	vanilla bean ice cream or whipped cream

PREPARATION

■ Heat the oven to 425°F. Toss the berries in a bowl with the sugar and tapioca and let stand 20 minutes. Pour the berry mixture into the baked pie shell.

■ Roll out the dough on a floured surface to about $1/8$ inch thick and 9 inches in diameter. Cut dough into $1/2$-inch strips and weave the strips into a lattice pattern on top of the berries. Brush the edge of the crust with beaten egg so that the dough will stick to the crust. Brush the lattice top with beaten egg, too. Place the bits of butter on the berries between the lattice strips.

■ Set the pie on a foil-covered baking sheet and gently wrap the foil over the pie rim to protect it from burning. Bake the pie on the top shelf in the oven for 15 minutes; reduce the heat to 375°F and bake about 30 minutes longer until the lattice top is golden brown. Remove to a wire rack to cool before cutting.

• EIGHT SERVINGS •

Atlanta 1996

EMILY LUCHETTI

Emily Luchetti is the nationally acclaimed executive pastry chef
for Stars and Stars Cafe, both in San Francisco, and Stars Oakville Cafe in
Napa Valley, California. Luchetti recently opened StarBake,
a retail bakery/coffee bar, and a wholesale bakery that supplies
Stars Restaurant and both cafes.

Emily's recipes have been featured in many magazines and in her first
book, *Stars Desserts*. She is currently working on a second book.

In 1990, Luchetti was rated by *The San Francisco Examiner* as
one of the top pastry chefs in the Bay Area. In 1992, the James Beard
Foundation hosted a reception honoring Luchetti as one of
the nation's premier women chefs. Most recently, *Chocolatier* magazine
named Luchetti one of the Top 10 Pastry Chefs in the
United States for 1994.

Caramel Pots de Crème

Chocolate Shortbread Stars with Mascarpone

Stars Lemon Bars

CARAMEL POTS DE CREME

. . . .

INGREDIENTS

1	*cup sugar*
¹/₄	*cup water*
2	*cups heavy whipping cream*
1	*cup milk*
6	*large egg yolks*

PREPARATION

■ Heat the oven to 300°F. In a large heavy-bottomed saucepan, dissolve the sugar in the water over low heat. Increase the heat to high and cook until the sugar is amber colored. Meanwhile, in a separate saucepan, scald the cream and milk over medium high heat. When the caramel mixture is a deep golden color, slowly pour the cream mixture into it, stirring constantly.

■ Whisk the egg yolks together in a large mixing bowl, then whisk the cream into the yolks. Strain and refrigerate the mixture until cool. Skim any bubbles off the top.

■ Pour the custard into six 6-ounce ovenproof ramekins. Place the ramekins in a baking pan and fill the pan half-full with hot water. (It is easier to fill the pan with water when it is already in the oven.) Cover with foil.

■ Bake the ramekins for about 50 minutes. When gently shaken, they should be set around the edges but still slightly creamy in the center. Cool on wire racks and then refrigerate several hours or overnight.

• SIX SERVINGS •

CHOCOLATE SHORTBREAD STARS WITH MASCARPONE

INGREDIENTS

Cookies

1	cup (2 sticks or 8 ounces) unsalted butter, softened
$^1/_2$	cup sugar
$1^1/_2$	cups all-purpose flour
$^1/_2$	cup cocoa powder, sifted
	pinch salt

Filling

1	cup mascarpone
1	tablespoon sugar
$^1/_4$	teaspoon vanilla extract

PREPARATION

■ *To prepare the cookies:* Beat the butter and sugar in the bowl of an electric mixer on low speed for 30 seconds. Add the flour, cocoa and salt; continue mixing on low speed for 3 to 5 minutes until the dough comes together in a cohesive mass.

■ Roll the dough on a lightly floured work surface to $^1/_4$ inch thick. With a 2-inch star-shaped cutter, cut out the cookies. Reroll the scraps and cut more cookies.

■ Place the cut-outs on parchment-lined baking sheets and chill for 1 hour in the freezer. Heat the oven to 250°F. Bake the shortbread 1 hour until firm.

■ *To prepare the filling and assemble:* Mix the mascarpone, sugar and vanilla in a small bowl. Spread about 1 tablespoon of mascarpone filling on half of the cookies. Put the remaining cookies on top, sandwiching the filling in the middle.

• MAKES EIGHTEEN •

Atlanta 1996

STARS LEMON BARS

. . . .

INGREDIENTS

2	*cups all-purpose flour, divided*
1/2	*cup powdered sugar plus extra for dusting top*
3/4	*cup (1 1/2 sticks or 6 ounces) cold unsalted butter, cut into pats*
3	*cups sugar*
6	*large eggs*
1	*cup plus 2 tablespoons freshly squeezed lemon juice*

PREPARATION

■ Heat oven to 325°F. Combine 1 1/2 cups flour and 1/2 cup powdered sugar in a mixing bowl. With a pastry blender or electric beaters, cut in the butter until the mixture is the size of small peas. Press the crust into the bottom of a 9x13-inch baking pan. Bake 20 to 25 minutes until golden. Decrease the oven temperature to 300°F.

■ Whisk together the sugar and eggs until smooth. Stir in the lemon juice and then the remaining 1/2 cup flour. Pour the lemon filling on top of the crust. Bake about 40 minutes until the filling is set.

■ Cool on a wire rack for 30 minutes, then cut into bars. Dust the tops with additional powdered sugar.

• MAKES TWENTY BARS •

CASSANDRA MITCHELL

Cassandra Mitchell, proprietor of the Diner in Yountville, California, has a philosophy for success based on simple ideas: delicious foods skillfully made from great basic ingredients, served in a friendly, casual and clean atmosphere at reasonable prices.

Honoring the traditional role of a diner in a small town, in 1976 Cassandra started serving some of the best breakfasts and lunches in the area, featuring recipes from family and friends. The food, which is made from scratch, uses all the produce she can grow as well as produce from local farmers. In 1978 she started serving dinners featuring Latin American specialties and American comfort foods.

Spinach Quesadillas with Avocado Salsa

Pumpkin Ginger Flan

SPINACH QUESADILLAS WITH AVOCADO SALSA

INGREDIENTS

¹/₄	cup (¹/₂ stick) butter, softened
4	garlic cloves, minced, divided
1	tablespoon finely chopped pickled jalapeño peppers
1	bunch fresh spinach, washed, tough stems removed, patted dry
1	cup finely grated asiago cheese
¹/₂	cup shredded Monterey Jack cheese
4	large flour tortillas

Avocado Salsa

1	medium avocado, peeled, seeded and cut into ¹/₂-inch cubes
1	tablespoon minced onion
1	tablespoon finely chopped fresh cilantro
2	tablespoons seasoned rice vinegar
1	tablespoon apple cider vinegar
¹/₄	teaspoon salt

PREPARATIONS

■ In a small bowl, blend together butter and half the minced garlic; reserve. In the bowl of a food processor, process remaining garlic and jalapeños until combined. Add spinach and process until finely chopped. Add both cheeses and process to a homogenized paste.

■ Spread 1 side of each tortilla with garlic butter. On the unbuttered sides of 2 tortillas, spread the spinach mixture. Place the remaining 2 tortillas on top to sandwich the spinach mixture in the middle. Heat a heavy skillet over medium-high heat. Add tortillas and cook, flipping tortillas once, until golden brown. Cut in wedges and serve with salsa.

■ *To prepare the salsa:* Gently mix together the avocado, onion, cilantro, rice vinegar, cider vinegar and salt.

• FOUR SERVINGS •

PUMPKIN GINGER FLAN

INGREDIENTS

1	*cup sugar*
¹/2	*cup water*
¹/4	*cup pared and finely grated fresh ginger*
1	*cup milk*
1	*cup half-and-half*
1¹/2	*cups cooked, puréed pumpkin*
¹/3	*cup sugar*
¹/4	*teaspoon salt*
3	*large eggs, slightly beaten*
2	*egg yolks, slightly beaten*

PREPARATION

- In a heavy skillet over medium-high heat, heat sugar, stirring frequently, until sugar melts. Stir in water and ginger; simmer about 10 minutes until syrup is golden brown. Strain through a wire mesh sieve; reserve ginger. Pour the hot syrup into the bottoms of eight 6-ounce ovenproof ramekins. Let cool.

- Heat oven to 325°F. Scald milk and half-and-half in a medium saucepan over medium-high heat. Remove pan from heat; add pumpkin, sugar, salt, reserved ginger and beaten eggs and yolks. Mix well, then pour mixture into ramekins, dividing evenly.

- Place ramekins in a large baking pan and pour in hot water to come halfway up the sides. Bake 45 minutes until custards are set. Remove from hot water and cool on wire racks.

• EIGHT SERVINGS •

BRADLEY OGDEN

Bradley Ogden is the chef and co-owner of the Lark Creek Inn,
Larkspur, California, and One Market Restaurant in San Francisco.
Bradley began his career at the Culinary Institute of America at Hyde Park,
New York, where he graduated with honors and was the
recipient of the Richard T. Keating Award, given to the student
most likely to succeed.

Bradley feels that the greatest influence on his cooking came
from his early exposure to fresh foods that are native to the United States.
His philosophy is "keep it simple, use the freshest ingredients
available and put them together in such a way that the flavors, colors
and textures combine to bring out the best in each other."

Consistent acclaim from reviewers and the public alike has
brought him worldwide recognition. Articles featuring his views on
American cuisine appear frequently in magazines, books
and on television.

Caesar Salad with Parmesan Croutons

Pot Roast with Herb Dumplings

Fresh Fruit Crisp

CAESAR SALAD WITH PARMESAN CROUTONS

INGREDIENTS

Dressing

2	garlic cloves, minced
1/2	teaspoon capers, minced
6	anchovy fillets, mashed
2	egg yolks
1/4	teaspoon dry mustard
2	tablespoons lemon juice
1/4	teaspoon salt
3/4	teaspoon cracked black pepper
1/2	cup olive oil

Parmesan Croutons

1/4	cup unsalted butter
6	small garlic cloves, peeled and crushed
2	cups French bread cut into 3/4-inch cubes
1/2	cup finely grated Parmesan cheese

Salad

2	heads romaine lettuce
1/2	teaspoon cracked black pepper
1/2	cup shaved Parmesan cheese

PREPARATION

■ *To prepare the dressing:* In a small bowl with a fork, mix the garlic, capers and anchovies into a paste. Beat in the egg yolks, mustard, lemon juice and salt and pepper. Whisking continuously, gradually add the olive oil. Refrigerate the dressing 30 minutes or longer.

■ *To prepare the croutons:* Heat the oven to 350°F. Melt the butter with the garlic in a small saucepan over medium heat. Remove from the heat and let stand 15 minutes. Strain the butter and discard the garlic. On a baking sheet, toss together the bread and garlic butter. Bake 15 minutes, stirring 2 or 3 times during baking. When the croutons are crisp and a deep golden brown, remove from the oven to a large bowl. Toss croutons with Parmesan cheese.

■ *To prepare the salad:* Tear the romaine leaves into 2-inch pieces. Wash, dry and refrigerate. Place the lettuce in a large bowl with black pepper. Toss the lettuce with dressing. Add the croutons and toss. Garnish with shaved Parmesan cheese.

• SIX SERVINGS •

POT ROAST WITH HERB DUMPLINGS

INGREDIENTS

Pot Roast

2	pounds boneless chuck roast
2	tablespoons all-purpose flour
2	tablespoons vegetable oil
1	each onion and carrot, chopped
4	cups beef stock
1	cup dry red wine
4	sprigs fresh thyme
1	bay leaf
4	round red-skinned potatoes
3	each carrots and parsnips
1	medium rutabaga
16	boiling onions, peeled
3	tablespoons olive oil

Herb Dumplings

1	cup all-purpose flour
2	teaspoons baking powder
1/4	teaspoon salt
2	tablespoons cold unsalted butter
2	tablespoons each finely chopped chives and parsley
1	large egg
1/3	cup milk

PREPARATION

■ *To prepare the pot roast:* Heat oven to 325°F. Trim excess fat from beef. Season with salt and pepper and dredge with flour. Heat vegetable oil in a heavy ovenproof casserole over medium heat. Add the roast and brown well on all sides. Remove the roast; add the chopped onion and carrot and cook until browned. Return the meat to the casserole with the stock, wine, thyme and bay leaf. Bring the liquid to a simmer, cover the pot and place in oven. Cook about 2 hours, turning the roast several times during cooking.

■ Cut the potatoes into 1-inch cubes. Pare and quarter the carrots and parsnips. Cut the rutabaga into 1-inch wedges. Toss the vegetables with the olive oil and season with salt and pepper. About 40 minutes before serving, place the vegetables in a roasting pan and roast in the oven until tender and lightly browned.

■ *To prepare the dumplings:* Sift together the flour, baking powder and salt into a mixing bowl. Cut in the butter until the mixture resembles coarse meal. Stir in the herbs. Beat the egg and milk together in a separate small bowl. Add 3/4 of the egg mixture to the dry ingredients, mixing with a fork to make a stiff dough. Add the remaining egg mixture if needed. Be careful not to overmix.

■ *To finish the dish:* When the roast is tender, remove it to a platter and keep warm. Strain the juices from the pot and skim off the fat. Return the juices to the pot and place on the stove over high heat; boil until reduced by half. Lower the heat to a simmer and drop the dumpling dough by teaspoons into the pot. Cover and simmer about 10 minutes or until a wooden pick inserted into the dumplings comes out clean. Surround the roast with the vegetables and the dumplings. Pour the remaining juices from the pot into a sauceboat.

• SIX SERVINGS •

FRESH FRUIT CRISP

. . . .

INGREDIENTS

Topping

³/₄	cup all-purpose flour
¹/₃	cup granulated sugar
¹/₃	cup packed brown sugar
¹/₄	teaspoon ground cinnamon
¹/₄	teaspoon salt
¹/₈	teaspoon ground ginger
6	tablespoons cold, unsalted butter

Fruit Filling

1¹/₂	pounds nectarines or peaches
1	pint-size basket blueberries or blackberries
¹/₄	cup sugar
2	tablespoons flour
	vanilla ice cream or lightly sweetened whipped cream

PREPARATION

■ *To prepare the topping:* In a mixing bowl, combine the flour, both sugars, cinnamon, salt, and ginger. Cut in the butter with a pastry blender or 2 forks until the mixture resembles coarse meal.

■ *To prepare the fruit filling and assemble:* Heat the oven to 400°F. Pit the nectarines and cut into ¹/₂-inch thick slices. Toss the nectarines in a bowl with the berries, sugar and flour. Place the fruit in a 1-quart baking dish. Scatter the topping over the fruit. Bake 25 to 30 minutes until the top is browned and the juices bubble up around the edge. Cool on a wire rack 15 minutes. Serve warm with ice cream or whipped cream.

• SIX SERVINGS •

WOLFGANG PUCK

Wolfgang Puck, a native of Austria, began his culinary training
at the early age of fourteen. After apprenticing in three-star restaurants
in France, he came to the Los Angeles area in 1973, where he drew
attention at the famous restaurant, Ma Maison. Wolfgang and his wife
and partner, Barbara Lazaroff, a designer, now own
five restaurants in California.

Wolfgang has authored three books: *Adventures in the Kitchen*,
The Wolfgang Puck Cookbook, and *Wolfgang Puck's
Modern French Cooking*.

Summer Tomato Soup

Chopped Vegetable Salad

Puck's Pizza

SUMMER TOMATO SOUP

INGREDIENTS

2	tablespoons olive oil
2	cups finely chopped onions
1	cup finely chopped carrots
1	cup finely chopped celery
6	garlic cloves, coarsely chopped
4	pounds tomatoes, seeded and coarsely chopped
1	cup chicken stock
1	bunch chervil, chopped
2	tablespoons finely chopped basil
1	cup heavy cream
	salt and white pepper
	crème fraîche and chopped chives for garnish

PREPARATION

■ Heat the oil in a large saucepan over medium heat. Add the onions, carrots, celery and garlic; sauté for 5 minutes, stirring occasionally. Add the tomatoes and cook 15 minutes. Add the chicken stock, chervil and basil; simmer 10 minutes. Pour ingredients into a blender or food processor and process until smooth.

■ Return the soup to the saucepan and stir in the cream; simmer 5 minutes. Strain the soup through a wire mesh sieve into a clean pot. Season with salt and white pepper. Ladle soup into heated bowls. Top with a dollop of crème fraîche and chopped chives.

• SIX SERVINGS •

CHOPPED VEGETABLE SALAD

. . . .

INGREDIENTS

Mustard Vinaigrette

1	tablespoon Dijon mustard
3	tablespoons sherry wine vinegar
1/2	cup almond or safflower oil
1/2	cup extra-virgin olive oil
	salt and white pepper

Salad

1	tablespoon olive oil
1/2	cup diced artichoke hearts
	salt and white pepper
1/2	cup diced green beans
1/2	cup diced carrots
1/2	cup diced radicchio
1/2	cup fresh corn kernels
1/2	cup diced red onion
1/2	cup diced celery
1/4	cup peeled, seeded, chopped tomato
1/2	cup diced avocado
4	teaspoons finely grated Parmesan cheese
1	cup mixed salad greens, torn into bite-size pieces

PREPARATION

■ *To prepare the vinaigrette:* Whisk together the mustard and vinegar in a small bowl with a wire whisk. Slowly whisk in the oils. Season to taste with salt and white pepper.

■ *To prepare the salad and serve:* Heat the olive oil in a small skillet over medium heat. Season the artichokes with salt and white pepper and sauté about 3 minutes until tender-crisp. Transfer to a large bowl.

■ Cook the beans and carrots in a pot of boiling salted water until tender-crisp; plunge into cold water to stop the cooking. Drain and add to the artichokes. Add the radicchio, corn, red onion and celery.

■ Just before serving, add the tomato and avocado. Toss with about 2/3 of the vinaigrette and the Parmesan cheese. Adjust seasonings to taste. Toss the remaining vinaigrette with the salad greens. Divide the salad greens among 4 plates. Mound the vegetables on top.

• FOUR SERVINGS •

PUCK'S PIZZA

. . . .

INGREDIENTS

1	*package active dry yeast*
1	*teaspoon honey*
³/₄	*cup warm water (105° to 115°F.), divided*
2³/₄	*cups all-purpose flour*
1	*teaspoon salt*
2	*tablespoons olive oil plus extra for brushing on the dough*
3	*cups (12 ounces) shredded mozzarella cheese, divided*
2	*cups (8 ounces) shredded Fontina cheese*
2	*cups (8 ounces) cooked artichoke hearts, sliced*
2	*cups (5 ounces) sliced, eggplant, grilled or sautéed*
4	*teaspoons finely grated Parmesan cheese*
1	*teaspoon chopped fresh oregano*

PREPARATION

■ In a small bowl, stir together the yeast, honey and ¹/₄ cup of the warm water. Combine the flour and salt in a mixer fitted with a dough hook. Add the oil, yeast mixture and remaining ¹/₂ cup water; mix to form a dough. Knead on low speed about 5 minutes. (If done by hand, knead about 8 minutes.) Turn the dough onto a floured work surface and knead by hand 2 to 3 minutes longer. Cover the dough with a damp towel and let rise in a warm area for about 30 minutes. (The dough will stretch when pulled.)

■ Divide the dough into 4 balls. Work each ball by pulling down the sides and tucking under the bottom of the ball. Repeat 4 or 5 times. On a smooth, unfloured surface, roll the ball under the palm of your hand until the dough is smooth and firm, about 1 minute. Cover with a damp towel and let rest 15 to 20 minutes.

■ Place a pizza stone in the oven and heat the oven to as hot as possible, 500°F for most ovens. Roll each ball into a 7- or 8-inch circle with the outer border a little thicker than the inner circle. Brush lightly with olive oil. Top with 2¹/₂ cups mozzarella cheese, Fontina cheese, artichokes, eggplant, Parmesan cheese, remaining mozzarella cheese and oregano, dividing evenly. Place the pizzas on the baking stone and bake 15 to 20 minutes until nicely browned.

• MAKES FOUR (SEVEN- TO EIGHT-INCH) PIZZAS •

Atlanta 1996

MICHEL RICHARD

Michel Richard began in the restaurant business at the young age
of thirteen, when he apprenticed in a restaurant that ran a pastry shop.
Six years later he moved to Paris, where he rose to the top chef
position at Gaston Lenotre's famous pastry shop. In May of 1974 he
moved to Manhattan to open Mr. Lenotre's first French pastry shop in the
United States. Soon, Michel felt the need to move on and opened
his own French pastry shop in Los Angeles. In no time, customers were
waiting in line halfway around the block to get a taste of
Michel's wonderful desserts.

Ten years later, with the creation of his first southern California
restaurant, Citrus, Michel Richard's life-long dream to cook in his own
restaurant was realized. Since then he has opened a number
of restaurants coast to coast.

He has received the James Beard Foundation's Who's Who Award,
the Ivy Award from *Restaurants and Institutions*, as well as many other
awards. In 1987, Citrus was voted the best restaurant in the
United States by *Traveler's* magazine.

Michel has had his own cooking show in Los Angeles, and has
been a guest on numerous TV and radio programs across the country.
His cookbook is *Michel Richard's Home Cooking with a French Accent*.

Tuna Burgers with Sesame Mayonnaise

Banana Soup with Rum Aspic

TUNA BURGERS WITH SESAME MAYONNAISE

INGREDIENTS

Sesame Mayonnaise

1	**cup mayonnaise**
1	**teaspoon toasted Oriental sesame oil**
1	**teaspoon Champagne vinegar or white wine vinegar**
1/2	**teaspoon ground cumin**
2	**drops hot pepper sauce**
1	**tablespoon sesame seeds**
2	**cups finely shredded savoy cabbage or green cabbage**

Tuna Burgers

1 3/4	**pounds tuna fillets, well chilled**
4	**garlic cloves, minced**
1/4	**cup olive oil, plus olive oil for pan frying**
4	**anchovies, minced**
1/4	**cup chopped fresh basil**
	salt and freshly ground black pepper to taste
	burger buns, split and lightly toasted

PREPARATION

■ *To prepare the sesame mayonnaise:* Mix together mayonnaise, sesame oil, vinegar, cumin, hot pepper sauce and sesame seeds in a medium mixing bowl. Add the cabbage and toss to coat.

■ *To prepare the tuna burgers and serve:* Trim off any dark, oily parts of the tuna. Thinly slice tuna and then chop it until the fish is the texture of hamburger and presses into a compact ball. Mix in the garlic, olive oil, anchovies, basil, salt and pepper. Divide the mixture into 4 balls and form into 1-inch thick patties.

■ Heat enough oil to coat the bottom of a heavy large nonstick skillet over medium-high heat. Add the tuna patties and cook for 1 minute per side for rare; about 1 1/2 minutes for medium rare. Place the burgers on one side of the split buns and top with sesame mayonnaise.

• FOUR SERVINGS •

BANANA SOUP WITH RUM ASPIC

INGREDIENTS

1	*cup dark rum*
1	*tablespoon sugar*
1	*envelope (¹/₄ ounce) gelatin*
4	*firm bananas*
2	*tablespoons lemon juice plus ¹/₂ teaspoon lemon juice*
1	*cup water*
1	*cup canned coconut milk*
1	*cup shredded coconut*
	mint sprigs for garnish

PREPARATION

■ Heat the rum and sugar in a small saucepan over medium-low heat. Add the gelatin and stir to dissolve. Pour the rum mixture into a shallow dish and refrigerate until firm.

■ Meanwhile, cut the bananas into ¹/₄-inch thick slices and toss gently with 2 tablespoons lemon juice to coat. Place the bananas, water and coconut milk in a medium saucepan; bring to a boil over medium-high heat. Lower the heat and simmer 1 minute. The bananas should still hold their shape. Strain through a wire mesh sieve, being careful not to mash the bananas; reserve bananas. Pour the liquid back into the saucepan and add the shredded coconut. Bring to a boil, lower the heat and simmer 1 minute. Strain liquid, discarding the coconut. Cool soup, then refrigerate to chill.

■ Finely chop the rum aspic and toss with remaining ¹/₂ teaspoon lemon juice. In the center of 4 shallow wide soup bowls, arrange the bananas overlapping in a tight circle. Pour the soup around the bananas. Spoon the aspic in the center of the circle. Garnish with mint sprigs.

• FOUR SERVINGS •

JOHN SEDLER

John Sedler grew up in Santa Fe, New Mexico, but his heritage
is deeply rooted in the pueblo of Abiquiu, to the north, where his
great-grandparents ran a ranch. In addition to spending time
in his grandmother's kitchen as she made tortillas, John had the good
fortune to travel at an early age. It was not long before cooking became a
passionate pursuit and he apprenticed with the legendary French
chef Jean Bertanou of L'ermitage.

John's first restaurant was Saint Estephe in Manhattan Beach, California.
The cooking, rooted in classic French technique, took a turn toward
"haute tamales" and Chimayo chiles filled with duxelles. Once
Saint Estephe took off, he opened Bikini and Abiquiu, both highly
successful restaurants in southern California.

The chef's professional accolades include being named to *Food & Wine*
magazine's Honor Roll of American Chefs and *Cook's Magazine*'s
Who's Who of Cooking in America. His book *Modern Southwest Cuisine*
will be available this fall.

Taos Caesar

Desert Sage & Garlic Roasted Chicken

TAOS CAESAR

. . . .

INGREDIENTS

Dressing

2	medium tomatoes, peeled and seeded
7	anchovy fillets
1	egg yolk
1	teaspoon minced garlic
1/2	cup red wine vinegar
1	cup plus 2 tablespoons olive oil
	salt and pepper to taste

Salad

6	hearts of Romaine lettuce
18	anchovy fillets
6	ounces Parmesan cheese, thinly shaved with a vegetable peeler
9	chives, cut in half
3/4	cup croutons
	chile powder

PREPARATION

■ *To prepare the dressing:* In a blender or food processor, process the tomatoes, anchovies, egg yolk, garlic and vinegar until blended and smooth. With the motor running, add the oil in a thin stream until all is incorporated. Season to taste with salt and pepper.

■ *To prepare the salad:* Pull the lettuce leaves from the core and arrange the spears on 6 chilled plates. Pour the dressing over the spears and arrange 3 chives and 3 anchovy fillets on each salad. Dust the croutons lightly with chile powder and scatter on top.

• SIX SERVINGS •

DESERT SAGE & GARLIC ROASTED CHICKEN

. . . .

INGREDIENTS

3	broiler-fryer chickens
1	cup corn bread crumbs
$^{1}/_{3}$	cup finely shredded fresh sage
$^{1}/_{3}$	cup finely sliced garlic
$^{1}/_{4}$	cup milk
1	teaspoon salt
1	teaspoon ground black pepper
	olive oil
	salt and black pepper to taste

Honey Baked Shallots

1	cup peeled shallots
$^{1}/_{2}$	cup peeled garlic cloves
2	tablespoons honey
2	tablespoons butter, melted
1	tablespoon finely shredded fresh sage
	salt and pepper to taste

PREPARATION

■ Heat oven to 375°F. Cut chickens in half down the backbone and remove the backbone and wing tips at the joint. Mix together the corn bread crumbs, sage, garlic, milk, 1 teaspoon salt and 1 teaspoon pepper in a mixing bowl. Carefully push a thin, even layer of stuffing between the meat and skin, dividing the stuffing equally among the chicken halves.

■ Brush chickens with oil; season with salt and pepper to taste. Place on oiled baking sheets and roast 35 to 45 minutes. Check for doneness by piercing the flesh of the leg with the tip of a knife. If the juices run clear, the chicken is done. Serve with honey baked shallots.

■ *To prepare the shallots:* Wrap all ingredients in aluminum foil and bake with the chicken in a 375°F oven until the chicken is done.

• SIX SERVINGS •

STEPHEN SIMMONS

Stephen Simmons and his wife Beth are the new owners
of Bubba's Diner in San Anselmo, California. As a chef/partner to
noted California chef Bradley Ogden, first at the Lark Creek Inn
in Larkspur, California, and then at One Market Restaurant
in San Francisco, Steve earned a reputation as a fine cook. In 1990
he was noted as a Rising Star of American Cuisine by the James Beard
Foundation and named one of the top Black Chefs in America
by the organization of 100 Black Men.

At Bubba's, Steve is having fun with down-home diner food—
great breakfasts, lunches and dinners—featuring dishes such
as biscuits and gravy, and blue-plate specials such as
barbecued ribs and coleslaw.

Lemon Mint Slush

Mashed Potato Pancakes with Fried Eggs

Biscuits & Gravy

LEMON MINT SLUSH

· · · · · · · · · · · · · · · ·

INGREDIENTS

3	lemons, peeled, white pith removed
3	cups orange juice
2	cups ice
1/2	cup sugar, or as needed to taste
2	cups sparkling water
1	tablespoon chopped mint
	mint sprigs for garnish

PREPARATION

■ Use a blender to make this drink in batches, dividing ingredients evenly. Slice lemons and add to the blender with orange juice, ice, sugar and sparkling water. Whirl until blended and slushy.

■ Taste for sweetness, adding more sugar if desired. Add the chopped mint and blend again. Pour into tall glasses and garnish with mint sprigs.

• SIX SERVINGS •

MASHED POTATO PANCAKES WITH FRIED EGGS

· · · · · · · · · · · · · · · ·

INGREDIENTS

4	medium russet potatoes
3	eggs
1/2	cup flour
1/4	cup cornmeal
1/4	teaspoon baking powder
	ground nutmeg
	salt and pepper
2	tablespoons butter
	fried or scrambled eggs

PREPARATION

■ Pare, cube and boil potatoes in lightly salted water until tender. Drain and allow to rest 20 minutes or longer. In a mixing bowl, mash potatoes with a potato masher or large fork. Add eggs, flour, cornmeal and baking powder; mix well. Season to taste with nutmeg, salt and pepper. Form into 6 patties about 1/2 inch thick.

■ Melt 1 tablespoon butter in a sauté pan; panfry 3 pancakes 4 to 5 minutes per side until browned and crisp. Keep warm. Repeat with remaining butter and pancakes. Serve with eggs.

NOTE: At Bubba's these Mashed Potato Pancakes are often served with sour cream, roasted tomato salsa and homemade applesauce.

• SIX SERVINGS •

BISCUITS & GRAVY

. . . .

INGREDIENTS

Biscuits

4	cups all-purpose flour
2	tablespoons baking powder
1½	teaspoons salt
½	cup (1 stick) butter, cut into pats
2	cups heavy cream

Gravy

2	slices bacon, diced
½	medium onion, diced
3	sprigs fresh thyme
¼	cup flour
1	cup milk
½	cup chicken stock
¼	cup coffee
	salt and pepper

PREPARATION

- *To make the biscuits:* Heat oven to 425°F. Combine flour, baking powder and salt in the bowl of a food processor; pulse to blend. Add butter; process until mixture is like cornmeal. With the machine running, add cream; process until mixture comes together as a dough.

- Pat dough onto a work surface to ½-inch thickness. Cut out with a 2½-inch biscuit cutter. Place on ungreased baking sheets. Bake 15 to 20 minutes until browned.

- *To make the gravy and serve:* Heat a cast-iron skillet over medium heat; add bacon, onion, thyme and flour; cook, stirring frequently, for 5 minutes. Add milk, chicken stock and coffee; cook stirring until mixture thickens into a gravy.

- Season with salt and pepper. Strain through a wire mesh sieve and serve with biscuits.

• TWELVE BISCUITS AND TWO CUPS GRAVY •

HIRO SONE & LISSA DOUMANI

Hiro Sone

For Hiro Sone, cooking is art. From the kitchen of his restaurant, Terra, located
in the heart of California's Napa Valley, Hiro's innovative palette mixes unexpected flavors
from Italy, France and the Orient, and his beautifully designed dishes emerge
as composed as paintings on canvas.

Hiro was born in Miyagi, about 200 miles north of Tokyo, into a farming family.
Although it was normally uncommon for a child to help in the kitchen, the demands of
his large family necessitated another set of hands. Thus when Hiro was five he
began cooking with his mother. After high school Hiro entered one of the world's most
prestigious cooking schools, the École Technique Hoteliere Tsuji in Osaka. After graduation,
he cooked in Tokyo and at Spago in Los Angeles. In 1988 Hiro launched Terra in
St. Helena, California, with pastry cook Lissa Doumani, who is his fiancée and partner.

Lissa Doumani

When Lissa was twelve she knew she wanted to own a restaurant. Born to a family of great
cooks and winemakers (her father is the owner of the venerable Stag's Leap Winery),
Lissa gained experience in the kitchens of La Cienega Restaurant and Spago, both in
Los Angeles. Lissa's pastry-chef history is evident in Terra's desserts. Though as hostess and
business manager she only has time to consult on the restaurant's dessert offerings,
they are things of which dreams are made: dense chocolate walnut brownie with bourbon
ice cream, exceptional sorbets served with a giant tuile, and fresh seasonal fruit tarts.

Mussel Saffron Soup with Caramelized Onions & Garlic Croutons

Grilled Veal Chops with Miso Sauce & Fried Eggplant

Crostata of Fruit

Atlanta 1996

MUSSEL SAFFRON SOUP WITH CARAMELIZED ONIONS & GARLIC CROUTONS

INGREDIENTS

Caramelized Onions

2	large onions
¼	cup butter

Garlic Croutons

	garlic cloves
12	pieces thinly sliced baguette, cut on the diagonal
	olive oil
	herbes de Provence

Soup

½	cup dry white wine
36	mussels, scrubbed clean, beards removed
1	tablespoon olive oil
1½	teaspoons minced garlic
⅓	cup finely chopped onion
2	cups chicken stock
2	cups heavy cream
½	cup tomato purée
	pinch saffron threads
	salt and pepper

PREPARATION

- *To prepare the caramelized onions:* Slice 2 large onions crosswise into thin rings. Sauté onions slowly in 4 tablespoons butter in a heavy sauté pan over medium-low heat until onions become very soft and then start to brown lightly.

- *To prepare the garlic croutons:* Rub cut garlic on both sides of 12 pieces thinly sliced baguette, cut on the diagonal. Brush with oil and sprinkle with herbes de Provence. Toast in a 350°F oven until crisp.

- *To prepare the soup and serve:* Bring wine to a simmer in a wide, shallow pot. Add mussels, cover pot and cook 3 to 5 minutes until mussels open; remove from heat. Set mussels aside; strain cooking liquid and reserve. In the same pan, heat oil, then add garlic and sauté until the mixture just starts to brown. Add onion and sauté until tender. Add reserved mussel cooking liquid, chicken stock, cream and tomato purée; bring to a boil. Stir in saffron and season with salt and pepper.

- Just before serving, put mussels and ½ cup of the caramelized onions into the broth; bring to a boil. Ladle soup into wide shallow bowls. Serve with garlic croutons.

• SIX SERVINGS •

GRILLED VEAL CHOPS WITH MISO SAUCE & FRIED EGGPLANT

. . . .

INGREDIENTS

Miso Sauce

1	cup Japanese red miso sauce
2	cups chicken stock
3	tablespoons sesame seeds
1/2	cup packed brown sugar
1/4	to 1/2 teaspoon red chili pepper flakes
1	tablespoon minced garlic
2	tablespoons finely chopped ginger

Veal Chops

1 1/2	cups basmati rice
	peanut oil
1	medium onion, diced
1	red bell pepper, seeded and diced
1	yellow bell pepper, seeded and diced
2	medium eggplants, cut into slender wedges
6	(approximately 9 ounces) veal chops
	salt and pepper
	cilantro sprigs and sesame seeds (white and black), for garnish

PREPARATION

■ *To prepare the Miso Sauce:* In a medium saucepan, combine miso sauce, chicken stock, sesame seeds, brown sugar, chili pepper flakes, garlic and ginger. Bring mixture to a boil; remove from heat and reserve.

■ *To prepare the veal chops and serve:* Cook basmati rice following packaged directions. Heat about 1 tablespoon oil in a sauté pan over medium heat; add onion and bell peppers; sauté until tender. Add sautéed vegetables to sauce.

■ Heat several more tablespoons of oil in sauté pan over high heat; add eggplant wedges and fry until tender.

■ Season veal chops with salt and pepper; grill over charcoal or gas to desired doneness.

■ Spoon rice into the center of each of 6 serving plates. Place veal chop on rice. Arrange eggplant on veal chop and ladle on sauce. Garnish with cilantro and sesame seeds.

• SIX SERVINGS •

Atlanta 1996

CROSTATA OF FRUIT

. . . .

INGREDIENTS

Almond Cream

1	cup (2 sticks) unsalted butter, softened
1	cup powdered sugar, sifted
2	teaspoons finely grated lemon zest
2	eggs
$^1/_2$	cup ground blanched almonds
$^1/_2$	teaspoon almond extract
$^1/_2$	teaspoon vanilla extract

Crostata of Fruit

$1^1/_2$	pounds puff pastry
6	medium peaches, nectarines, pears or apples
$^1/_3$	cup sugar
	vanilla ice cream or sweetened crème fraîche

PREPARATION

■ *To prepare the almond cream:* In a mixing bowl with electric beaters, beat butter and powdered sugar until light and fluffy. Beat in lemon zest, eggs, almonds and extracts.

■ *To prepare crostata of fruit and serve:* Heat oven to 325°F. Cut puff pastry into eight 5-inch circles. Spread 2 tablespoons of the almond cream to within $^1/_2$ inch of the edge of each puff pastry circle.

■ Pare fruit and slice about $^1/_8$ inch thick. Lay the fruit on the cream overlapping slightly to form a circular flower pattern. Sprinkle the edges of pastry with sugar. Place on a 10x15-inch baking sheet.

■ Bake 20 to 30 minutes until edges are golden and underside is fully cooked. Serve with ice cream or crème fraîche.

• EIGHT SERVINGS •

Nutrition, the Athlete, and You

WHAT WILL THE ATHLETES be eating at the 1996 Centennial Olympic Games? It depends: Is she a 98-pound gymnast, or is he a 250-pound weight lifter?

Dr. Ann Grandjean

When it comes to nutrition and athletes, one size definitely does not fit all. That's why food suppliers will be providing the athletes in Atlanta with a wide variety of foods around the clock— from low-calorie to energy-packed, from leisurely dining to quick service. It will be up to the athletes to pick and choose the right combination of foods to meet their unique nutritional needs and help them achieve their best performances.

One of the food suppliers, McDonald's, a Sponsor of the Games, will be the first quick-service restaurant to serve athletes in an Olympic Village. Their six locations will offer many McDonald's favorites, plus additional options such as a salad bar, carrot sticks, low-fat yogurt, fresh fruit, and bottled water.

There are several principles guiding the athlete's selection of foods. "The best diet," states Dr. Ann Grandjean, director of the International Center for Sports Nutrition (ICSN) and consultant to the United States Olympic Committee, "is one that keeps you well hydrated, provides adequate calories, and supplies the right amounts of the fifty-plus nutrients that your body needs."

This formula is achieved by consuming a variety of foods on a daily basis. If nutrients are missing or inadequate over time, there can be a negative effect on both health and athletic performance. "This," she cautions, "could mean the difference between winning and losing."

Good nutrition isn't just for athletes. It's important to each and every one of us, particularly children, who require both good food and adequate exercise to help them develop healthy hearts, lungs, and bones.

As a tool to help families set up basic ground rules for healthful eating, Dr. Grandjean points to the Food Guide Pyramid, developed by the United States Department of Agriculture. The pyramid features five food groups that should be eaten every day. Of the five, none is more or less important than the others; if one is left out, vital nutrients will be missed.

The ICSN provides the following tips for teaching children the importance of good nutrition and regular exercise.

◆ **Plan meals with the five basic food groups in mind. For example, to fit two servings of fruit into a day, slice a banana over cereal for breakfast and pack an apple into a lunch.**

◆ **Encourage family outings that involve physical activity, such as hiking, biking, and swimming.**

◆ **Watch for weight gains and losses in your children, but never put a child on a diet of any sort, including a heart-healthy diet, without consulting a family physician or pediatrician.**

◆ **Be a good role model by participating in your own nutrition and exercise program.**

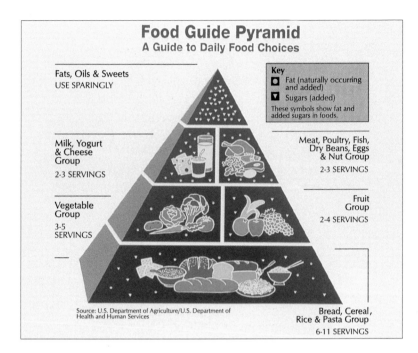

Food Guide Pyramid
A Guide to Daily Food Choices

Fats, Oils & Sweets
USE SPARINGLY

Key
□ Fat (naturally occurring and added)
▼ Sugars (added)

These symbols show fat and added sugars in foods.

Milk, Yogurt & Cheese Group
2-3 SERVINGS

Meat, Poultry, Fish, Dry Beans, Eggs & Nut Group
2-3 SERVINGS

Vegetable Group
3-5 SERVINGS

Fruit Group
2-4 SERVINGS

Source: U.S. Department of Agriculture/U.S. Department of Health and Human Services

Bread, Cereal, Rice & Pasta Group
6-11 SERVINGS

Using the information below, calculate the approximate number of calories you need to eat each day in order to maintain your desired weight. This will help you determine the appropriate number of servings each day from the five food groups.

A moderately active *female* requires approximately 17 calories a day per pound of body weight. For example, a 110-pound female will require about 110 x 17, or 1,870 calories, a day. (A less active female will require fewer calories—about 16 calories a day per pound.)

A moderately active *male* requires approximately 19 calories a day per pound of body weight. For example, a 145-pound male will require about 145 x 19, or 2,755 calories, a day. (A less active male will require fewer calories—about 17 calories a day per pound.)

	Lower	Moderate	Higher
Approximate calorie needs	1,600	2,200	2,800
Bread group (servings)	6	9	11
Vegetable group (servings)	3	4	5
Fruit group (servings)	2	3	4
Milk group (servings)	2–3	2–3	2-3
Meat group (ounces)	5	6	7

Page No	Recipe Title (Approx Per Serving)	Cal	Prot (g)	Carbo (g)	T Fat (g)	% Cal from Fat	Chol (mg)	Fiber (g)	Sod (mg)
37	Lemon-Herb Chicken Cooked Under a Brick	524	54	6	32	55	163	1	154
44	Marinated Swordfish Steaks *	140	23	0	5	72	45	0	104
45	Steamed Boston Brown Bread with Raisins	80	2	18	<1	4	<1	1	108
57	Red Wine & Cassis Strawberries	133	<1	22	<1	12	0	3	3
59	Angel Food Cake & Frozen Yogurt with Strawberry-Rhubarb Syrup	412	10	87	2	5	6	4	472
64	Shrimp & Fettuccine	607	20	69	26	39	117	3	871
70	Oven-Roasted Vegetable Chowder	179	3	33	5	24	0	5	69
74	Pacific Time Pâte Imperiale	28	2	5	<1	11	9	1	29
75	Napa Kim Chee (per cup)	196	2	53	<1	1	0	1	775
81	Blackberry Preserves	44	<1	11	<1	1	0	1	<1
88	Butter Lettuce Salad	175	1	4	18	90	0	1	6
92	Catfish Stew & Rice	428	30	64	7	15	68	10	403
98	Chilled Yogurt Soup	58	4	9	1	17	4	1	48
98	Broiled Red Snapper with Mango & Vidalia Onion Salsa	211	36	10	2	11	64	1	79
102	Mexican Sangria	182	<1	28	<1	<1	0	<1	7
109	Broiled Whitefish	312	44	0	14	41	140	0	118
111	Sweet-Herb-Seared Halibut with Three-Bean Salad	557	55	21	28	46	75	6	131
112	Fillet of Yellow Tail Snapper Steamed in Napa Cabbage & Scallion Vinaigrette	533	50	11	32	54	85	3	195
117	Walnut, Beet, Grapefruit & Endive Salad	309	5	26	23	62	0	6	101
125	Mango, Sweet Pepper & Grilled Red Onion Salad	196	2	26	11	46	0	4	13
126	Pork Loin Chops in Tomato Mushroom Sauce with Polenta	389	29	34	16	36	71	6	1317
130	Orange & Jicama Salad	100	2	22	1	12	0	4	3
132	Red Chile Sauce	12	1	1	1	48	3	<1	28
138	Chile Slaw	137	3	14	8	52	17	3	36
148	Ruby Red Grapefruit & Tequila Sorbet	177	1	34	<1	1	0	<1	3
164	Salmon Salad with Sun-Dried Tomato Vinaigrette	215	15	7	14	56	40	2	109
165	Roasted Breast of Chicken with Fava Beans, Grilled Portabello Mushrooms & Tarragon	369	36	31	11	27	89	7	160
168	Rattlesnake Salsa	4	<1	1	<1	29	0	<1	14
169	Salad of Raw Artichokes, Fava Beans & Parmesan Cheese	601	38	87	16	22	9	29	480
172	Grilled Figs, Chanterelles & Prosciutto (per fig)	192	4	12	15	28	6	2	155
184	Fresh Fruit Crisp	364	3	63	12	30	31	4	98
194	Desert Sage & Garlic Roasted Chicken	794	101	22	32	37	320	2	784
196	Lemon Mint Slush	129	1	32	<1	2	0	1	2

* Nutritional profile for this recipe does not include the marinade.

CHEF INDEX

RECIPE INDEX

Atlanta 1996

GENERAL INDEX